Nurturing Discussions and Practices

Nurture Nature, Yourself and Your Relationships

Rev. Dr. LoraKim Joyner and Gail Koelln

Published by One Earth Conservation
Hollis Hills, NY
www.oneearthconservation.org

ISBN: 978-0-9992070-2-4
First Edition First Printing

If making a copy of this book or the individual guides, please consider donating $10 to One Earth Conservation at
 https://www.oneearthconservation.org/donate.
All proceeds go to directly to helping the people and the parrots of the world.

Cover Design Copyright 2019 © by Gail Koelln.

This book is dedicated to all the nurturers and naturers who have been part of our programs over the years, guiding each other into letting the soft animal of our bodies love what they love, and to the other beings who welcome us into the family of living things.

Table of Contents

Introduction

Nurture Nature Program 1

Nurture Nature Communities 3

How to Use these Guides 4

The Guides*

Ellen Compassionate Communication (**EI**, SI, MI) 7

Bev Compassion and Empathy (EI, SI, **MI**) 23

Pat Awe and Wonder (EI, **MI**, SpI) 45

NO Dec meeting Bev M. Evil and Harm (EI, **MI**, **EcI**, SpI) 67

Connie Birding for Life (**EcI**, SpI) 91

June Nature Poetry (**EcI**, SpI) 109

Gail Spiritual Animals (SpI) 127

Freedom and Liberation (**EcI**) 149

Appendices

Plutchik's Wheel of Emotions 181

Universal Needs 182

Five Intelligences Graphic 183

Multispecies Primer 184

Wild Walks Guide 186

One Earth Conservation 188

The Authors 189

*Legend: Emotional Intelligence (**EI**), Social Intelligence (**SI**) Multispecies Intelligence (**MI**), Ecological Intelligence (**EcI**), Spiritual Intelligence (**SpI**). Items in bold are emphasized in the guide next to which they appear as such.

"It all begins and ends in beauty" (LoraKim Joyner)

INTRODUCTION

We are convinced, now more than ever, that to gain the powers of solidarity, resilience, and resistance we have to come together in local communities that are committed to and claimed by the biotic community in which they are embedded. Only in this way can we mourn, learn, and have sufficient focus and wisdom to build a new way, even as the old way crumbles around us. These guides, given the risks and challenges of these times, are meant to augment community formation and personal transformation and commitment, whether you are beginning something new or use these guides for an already existing community, family, or organization. They are meant to be broadly nonsectarian, but also can be adopted by particular religious or spiritual institutions and endeavors. They are adaptable for a wide variety of circumstances, with the overall goal of supporting the health of individuals, relationships, and communities of all species. They will:

- Deepen your connection to nature, animals, self, and others
- Grow your resilience
- Augment your advocacy, justice work, and compassionate care of individuals of all species
- Develop community and relationships
- Foster your loving animal nature
- Cultivate acceptance of self and others of all species

Topics selected best address themes related to human and multispecies flourishing. We emphasize the multispecies component because this is often overlooked in other spiritual, religious, health, and justice approaches. The foundation of all these guides is the concept of Nonviolent Communication (Compassionate Communication), founded by Marshall Rosenberg, because of its emphasis on individual needs, and not ideology, politics, or categories. Understanding needs, desires, and motivations help us to unweave how we negatively categorize beings, so that we can grow our sense of worth of individuals of all species, including ourselves!

These guides represent and supplement the Nurture Nature Program of One Earth Conservation.

Nurture Nature Program

One Earth Conservation's Nurture Nature Program (NNP) aims to inspire, motivate, educate, and support people to take care of themselves, their organizations, other individuals of all species, and the biotic community as a whole by developing their awareness and

1

understanding of nature, especially human nature as it relates to all of nature. Participants are then able to leverage this awareness and understanding to nurture themselves and others, leading to the growth of more efficient and resilient nurturers and naturers for the benefit of all life.

There is no final arriving, for nurturing and naturing exists along a continuum. No matter where you are or under which circumstances you were born or developed, you can move along the continuum, ever growing your capacity and resilience to be nourished, and to nurture nature. Nurturing Nature is a lifetime practice ever refining and more greatly embodying the understanding that all beings are interconnected to each other in beauty, worth, and well-being.

One Earth's Vision of Interbeing

1. All individuals of all species have inherent worth and dignity (all bodies are beautiful, have worth, and matter).

2. All individuals of all species are connected to each other in worth and beauty and well-being.

3. We are also connected in harm. There is no beauty without tragedy. What is done to another, is done to all of us.

4. Embracing this reality, humans grow in belonging to this wondrous planet and the life upon it, and so embraced and nurtured, can nurture in return.

5. This reality of *interbeing* makes us both powerful and vulnerable, therefore, we need each other to grow and to heal as much as possible.

6. Humans are a plastic species, and can change, both individually and as families, organizations, communities, and societies. We can become more effective and joyful nurturers and "naturers." This is hard, deep, intentional, and a lifetime's work.

Our Five Natures with Intention and Intelligence

There are multitudinous facets to human nature, many of which can be intentionally nurtured so as to make individuals and groups greater nurturers and naturers. The NNP emphasizes the following five natural intelligences of human nature:

Our Natural Intelligence	Using Our Natural Intelligence to...
Emotional Intelligence	Be in Beauty
Social Intelligence	Be with the Other in Beauty
Multispecies Intelligence	Be the Other
Ecological Intelligence	Be the Relationships
Spiritual Intelligence	Be All

Each of these intelligences interconnect through a primary understanding of how individuals from unicellular to complex social vertebrates respond to stimuli in their environment by "moving away" from harm or discomfort and "moving towards" benefit and satisfaction. Each individual has a subjective experience and makes decisions about what to do, so as to meet their needs. For some species, we can easily term these subjective experiences as emotions. These emotions are the motivators for response to the environment (behavior). We can therefore come to greater understanding and acceptance of the inherent worth and dignity of all beings by seeking to know their subjective experience and how it relates to behavior meant to meet needs. In other words, what is another feeling and needing? By answering this we can have greater choice regarding how to have deeper connections with nature – ours, other's, and the earth's. With this deeper connection, we foster a greater sense of belonging, and in that welcoming embrace of life, we welcome others into the family of beings through compassionate and empowered action.

We can maximally grow these intelligences embedded in a multispecies community, and hence, we intentionally gather in Nurture Nature Communities, for which these guides were developed.

Nurture Nature Communities

We are connected to all of life, interwoven with the many in our biotic communities, and in that web of beauty and belonging we are nurtured so that we may nurture all of nature. Embracing and embraced by reality, we practice nurturing and naturing to build resilience to save ourselves and save our world. We can do this with intention, knowing that humans can change. We do this in community so that we can assert the beauty of every part of existence, including ourselves. We are the beauty we behold around us. Nourished and sustained by strands of interconnecting beauty that weave the interdependent web of life, we can in turn offer ourselves fully to life, and to the task of nurturing others. We need each other so that we can go into each day fully living, nourished no matter what, nourishing no matter what. For this reason, we use the guides to build communities that nurture and "nature."

These communities can be officially and closely integrated with the Nurture Nature Program of One Earth Conservation in hope that we network across a greater region with more people involved. An affiliated Nurture Nature Community is a group of people inspired by One Earth's Vision. So inspired, this group commits to grow their capacity in the five intelligences through learning, practice, and experience. The community stays connected to One Earth and other One Earth Communities by engaging in similar and simultaneous learning, practices, and experiences. These communities are strongly co-creative, as each community must arise out of ongoing relationships and the species and biomes that make up the multispecies community. Each Nurture Nature Community uses these guides in way that answers the question: What is it that is ours to do? To officially connect, follow these steps:

1. Contact us at info@oneearthconservation.org so we can guide and support you
2. Sign up for One Earth's newsletter with Nurture Nature tips and news about upcoming events and our conservation efforts in Latin America.
3. Go to our website and receive a free Nurture Nature Guide at http://www.oneearthconservation.org
4. Sign up for future webinars and other Nurture Nature events at http://www.oneearthconservation.org
5. Take courses through our online Nurture Nature Academy at http://www.nurture-nature.thinkific.com

How to Use These Guides

Please use these guides for your community regardless of whether you affiliate with the Nurture Nature Program or not. You can also use these guides to support your individual spiritual, mindfulness, or growth practices, though we really want to emphasize the need of the world today for people committed to local communities and biotic communities. We suggest that each member of your community or gathering obtain a copy of this entire workbook because of the supplemental material, however, you are free to copy each individual guide for distribution. If you do so, we invite you to offer a donation to One Earth Conservation to support communities and to produce these and future guides.

This workbook contains eight guides that will last most groups about a year, given the probability that most groups use one guide per month, and may very well skip some months. We suggest that the community agree to meet for a year, because of the benefits of time for developing relationships, community formation, understanding of the material, and embodiment of the concepts. The cognitive portions of our brains are fast learners, but the subconscious and limbic systems are less so. More time put into this work will result in better outcomes.

Each guide begins with an agenda on how to use the guide in a gathering that lasts approximately 1.5 hours. We suggest augmenting this reflection/discussion time with an outdoor activity, such as outdoor stretches, a walking meditation, or a Wild Walk (see the Wild Walk Guide in the Appendix). For each gathering, assign a facilitator ahead of time who will keep the group on track and help people to share the time and to be open, inviting, and inclusive with their comments. Facilitation is supported by other Nurture Nature activities that provide background and practice, including publications, live and recorded webinars, and the Nurture Nature Academy. Also, please note that where links to webpages are included, we have made them hyperlinks, so readers using the pdf version of the book can access the webpages as easily as possible. If you could like us to send you a pdf file of this book, please email this request to info@oneearthconservation.org. We suggest that each member of your group read the guide and engage in activities/exercises before you meet to be able to get the most out of the guide.

Each of the eight guides cover readings, reflections, activities, exercises, and resources. We also suggest that copies be distributed of the handouts that includes a graphic of the five intelligences, as well as a framework for considering other species in our human development (in the Appendix starting on page 181). We emphasize this, because of the lack of multispecies awareness in general across most societies and because well-being is interconnected – we need the individuals of all species to flourish in our biotic and human communities.

These eight guides support growth in the five intelligences – Emotional (EI), Social (SI), Multispecies (MI), Ecological (EcI) and Spiritual (SpI) – and all of the intelligences directly include multispecies intelligence. The Table of Contents list which intelligences are emphasized, although as you can see from the Five Intelligences Graphic in the Appendix that the five intelligences are interwoven, with no clear delineation between them. The intelligences that each guide emphasizes are listed, with the prominent one in bold:

Compassionate Communication (**EI**, SI, MI)
Compassion and Empathy (EI, SI, **MI**)
Awe and Wonder (EI, **MI,** SpI)
Evil and Harm (EI, **MI, EcI,** SpI
Birding for Life (**EcI,** SpI)
Nature Poetry (**EcI,** SpI)
Spiritual Animals (SpI)
Freedom and Liberation (**EcI**)

We begin with the one on Compassionate Communication to sustain the group's efforts in supporting each other with honesty and empathy. It also emphasizes how important is seeing the interconnecting beauty between self and all of life. We need to grow our self awareness, empathy, and acceptance if we are to grow more deeply connected to and accepting of life around us. More guides may be made available on topics such as Animality and Worth, Love, Death, Justice, Mourning, and Parenting. These will be made available one at a time and once all are produced, compiled into a Volume II Nurture Nature Guide. Please send in topics that you believe would be of interest to you and others.

The Authors

Rev. LoraKim Joyner, DVM: LoraKim combines her experience as a wildlife veterinarian, Unitarian Universalist minister, and Certified Trainer in Nonviolent Communication to address the importance of both human and nonhuman well being in living a deeply meaningful and vibrant life, as well as caring for self, family, relationships, organizations, and life all around us. She serves as a Community Minister affiliated with the Community Unitarian Universalist Church at White Plains, and Co-Director of One Earth Conservation. As an adjunct professor at the Meadville Lombard Theological School, LoraKim teaches "Multispecies and Ecological Ministry, Theology, and Justice" and "Compassionate Communication." She is an inspiring speaker, leading workshops and webinars all over the country in Compassionate Communication and Nurturing Nature. With over 30 years of experience working in Latin America, LoraKim currently leads projects in Guatemala, Honduras, Nicaragua, Guyana, and Paraguay. You can read about her life and work in her memoir, *Conservation in Time of War*.

Gail Koelln, MS: For as long as she can remember, animals have nurtured Gail through their beauty and wonder, and she loves to care for them. As a child, Gail was inspired by Jane Goodall and wanted to grow up to be a zoologist like her. She earned a Master's degree in Zoology, but for various reasons left the field. However, over many years Gail volunteered for the Wildlife Conservation Society, NYC Sierra Club, Gotham City Networking (leading their Gotham Green group), and Climate Reality Project. As a grant writing professional for more than 20 years, she has worked with a number of animal welfare, wildlife, and environmental organizations. After Gail met LoraKim in 2014, she finally found her life's work serving as the Co-Director of One Earth Conservation.

General Resources

- One Earth Conservation. https://www.oneearthconservation.org/

- Nuture Nature Program. https://www.oneearthconservation.org/nurture-nature

- Nurture Nature Academy. www.nurture-nature.thinkific.com

- LoraKim Joyner. *Liberating Wings: Freeing People and Parrots Together*. https://www.nocageisbigenough.org/resources-for-action

- Marshall Rosenberg. *Nonviolent Communication: A Language of Life.*

Guide #1: Compassionate Communication

Growing our emotional and social intelligence to see the beauty within and without

Guide #1 Table of Contents

FORMAT FOR NURTURE NATURE COMMUNITY · 10

READINGS
Main Reading: The Path of Nurturing Yourself and Other: Empathy and Honesty · · · · · · · · 11
Main Reading: Natural Intelligences for Honesty, Empathy, and Compassion · · · · · · · · · · · 15

REFLECTIONS
Reflection Questions · 17

NURTURE NATURE PRACTICES
Nurturing Ourselves: Go For A Beauty Walk (every day for a week) · · · · · · · · · · · · · · · · · 18
Deepening and Sharing Ourselves: Empathy through Other-Empathy · · · · · · · · · · · · · · · · 20
Moving from Inner to Outer Work · 21

RESOURCES · 21

Published by One Earth Conservation, www.oneearthconservation.org
info@oneearthconservation.org

Please help us to continue to provide free resources for the public, such as this guide, by giving a tax-deductible donation to One Earth Conservation at: https://www.oneearthconservation.org/donate
All proceeds go to directly to helping the people and the parrots of the world.

Thanks to Rev. Meredith Garmon and Community Unitarian Universalist Congregation (http://www.cucwp.org/) for compiling some of these materials as part of their Journey Group program.

Photo credits: page 11 A. Elizabeth, page 13 Valerii Tkachenko

Format for Nurture Nature Community

We speak and listen deeply with our hearts and minds, allowing each to speak without interruptions, questions, or advice (unless solicited). The facilitator will help guide us in this so we can make the deepest connections possible to ourselves, others, earth, and earth's beings.

Arriving/Warm Up

As you arrive, make a name tag and write a word or draw a picture of something that is beautiful to you.

Opening Words

"What a Wonderful World" – Louis Armstrong (https://www.youtube.com/watch?v=B8WHKRzkCOY)

Check In

How is it with you today?
Where do you see beauty?

Our Nurture Nature Practice (embodiment) - (Choose either practices #1, # 2)

Shared Exploration

What do you make of the readings? How might they help you and others? (Compassionate Communication, Nonviolent Communication, Natural Intelligences)
Choose one or more Reflection Questions to share with one another (page 10)

Next Steps

Any group commitments for changes/actions to take together?
Facilitator, location, and subject of next meeting
Next community gathering -

Check Out

From everything we've shared during this time together, what overall message stands out for you?
Are you inspired to make any changes or take any actions?
What gratitudes do you have for our time together?

Closing Words

"Everything begins and ends in beauty" (Rev. Dr. LoraKim Joyner)

MAIN READINGS

The Path of Nurturing Yourself and Other: Empathy and Honesty
Rev. Dr. LoraKim Joyner

You are a manuscript of a divine letter.
You are a mirror reflecting a noble face.
This universe is not outside of you.
Look inside yourself;
everything that you want,
you are already that.
If you are irritated by every rub, how will your mirror be polished?
– Rumi

Both empathy and honesty are foundational in Compassionate Communication (CC), Nonviolent Communication (NVC), and Emotional/Social/Multispecies Intelligence (EI/SI/MI). Compassionate Communication /Nonviolent Communication are both a spiritual practice and communication art tool at the same time. Both rewire our brains so that we embody compassion for self and others ever more quickly and automatically, and under times of greater duress and ambiguity. Nonviolent Communication was founded by Marshall Rosenberg and is international in scope (www.cnvc.org). NVC, CC, and EI/SI are frameworks help us develop connection to self and others, in part because we see how others are so much like us, and also so much different. No matter the difference we are all connected to the beauty of life. Developing our emotional intelligence helps us achieve greater connection to self and other acceptance.

Empathy of others and self-empathy are interconnected: each facilitates and reinforces the other. The beauty and needs we deny ourselves we will end up also denying to others – and what we deny to others we will end up also denying to ourselves. The more "we shine our mirror" of doing our work of seeing our own inner beauty, the more we are able to reflect the beauty of others, and bring peace and possibility into the world.

"Love the world as yourself, and you will be able to care for it properly."

– Lao Tzu, *The Tao Te Ching*

What matters most is how you see yourself.

Louie Bryan M. Lapal

If we don't love and care for ourselves fiercely, we cannot be fierce advocates for this wondrous world and her beings. Taking time and energy to understand oneself, and to then to manage the outcomes of this understanding is not a selfish act, but a self-full blessing that nurtures us, and hence the many others to whom our souls are deeply connected.

"Self-Empathy: Deep and compassionate awareness of one's own inner experience"

– Marshall Rosenberg

Self-empathy means identifying and considering our feelings and needs without judgment, and it is no easy task. We all grew up in a culture where blame, domination, judgment, bullying, and power over others were the methods that were modeled for us as ways to meet our needs. If our needs were not being met, it was surely the fault of someone else – someone fundamentally wrong, at least in some aspects of their being. The tools we have for thinking about others are also the tools with which we think about ourselves: so, we also see ourselves as basically flawed and lacking. These negative judgments harm our well-being, sap our energy, divert us from our goals and dreams, decrease our happiness and effectiveness, and affect our health.

11

"But the irony of affective empathy is that it requires being really good at listening to one's self. A person has to be able to identify his or her own feelings to notice how they're resonating with someone else's."
– Andrew Price

Self-empathy is necessary for our individual flourishing, and is a hallmark of emotional intelligence. Emotional intelligence is the awareness of one's emotions and the ability to manage them.While a person's emotional intelligence is influenced by genetic predisposition and by encouragement (or discouragement) in the early years, almost all of us, whatever our genes or age, have the capacity to increase, at least a little bit, our emotional intelligence – and thus our self-understanding and care.

As animals, we have emotions. Almost constantly, we are having one or more emotions. The fact that we are having them, though, doesn't mean we know we are having them. Nor does it mean we know which one(s) we are having.

We have to bring to higher consciousness the emotions, feelings, moods, and body states our mind and body is communicating. The limbic system, the location in our brains through which emotions communicate to our mind, body, and higher cognitive functions, is a slow learner. It takes repetition and practice to grow awareness of emotions and to manage them. If we can do this, we have greater choices on how to think, feel, and act. Nonviolent communication is not about "getting it right" or "getting rid of uncomfortable emotions," it is about increasing our choices. To be fully alive means feeling everything – the comfortable,

Guide #1: Compassionate Communication

the uncomfortable. Don't push any of it away. Whatever you're trying to ignore or deny or suppress, that's what you're dead to. Life isn't about what you like. It's about what you can open yourself to – attend to, learn from, love.

The more honest you can be with seeing yourself for who you are, which means not suppressing your feelings, the more tenderly honest you can be with others. You can also more clearly communicate what you really mean to in a way that helps build connections and trust with another, and can help you be precise, open, and curious about requests you have of others and how they respond to you. If you suspect that your honest message will be painful, be ready to offer empathy to the receiver. Also, couple your honest messages with clear and doable requests in the moment.

Being honest with others helps us live authentically and be more deeply connected to life, not matter how the other people around us react. Honesty, authenticity, and connection most likely communicates self- and other-acceptance, which results more likely in being listened to and understood.

In summary, honesty and empathy helps us live better with ourselves and our world, and in so doing, nurtures our relationships and communications so that all have a greater chance for flourishing.

Beyond our ideas of right-doing and wrong-doing,
there is a field. I'll meet you there.
When the soul lies down in that grass,
the world is too full to talk about.
Ideas, language, even the phrase 'each other'
doesn't make sense anymore.
– Rumi

Guide #1: Compassionate Communication

Natural Intelligences for Honesty, Empathy, and Compassion

Basically, translate everything into feeling (emotions) and needs (motivators) language. This decreases judgment, opens us to a curious wonder of others, and grows our connection to and acceptance of life.

Emotional Intelligence

Emotional Intelligence (EI) is the ability to identify, assess, and have choice around the emotions of oneself, of others, and of groups. The term "emotion" broadly includes body states, affect (subconscious rapid emotional response), feelings, emotions, and moods. Emotions are a common factor in many species, and we all have them for a reason; they are a part of our neurophysiology that motivates us to move towards satisfaction, and away from harm. Emotions are neither good nor bad, but exist as part of evolution, tying us to nature and to others. The greater awareness we have of these emotions, the greater chance that we have choice around our behavior that often is subconsciously directed by our emotions. Even when we can't have choice in the moment, or even days later, EI allows us to be present with the emotions instead of pushing them away, or judging others or ourselves for having them. Life is not about feeling comfortable, but about feeling everything, and in that space, we come completely alive, and more whole and compassionate.

One of the most beneficial emotions for our health, and one that leads to self- and other compassion, is empathy. Self-empathy is curiosity and openness to one's emotions (feelings, mood, affect) and needs (motivations that cause us to move towards or away from circumstances), resulting in us having choice in our behavior and thinking. Empathy for others and self-empathy are interconnected: each facilitates and reinforces the other. The beauty and needs that we deny ourselves we will also end up denying to others – and what we deny to others we will also end up denying to ourselves. The more "we shine our mirror," that is, doing the work of seeing our own inner beauty, the more we are able to reflect the beauty of others, and bring peace and possibility into the world. If we don't love and care for ourselves fiercely, we cannot be fierce advocates for this wondrous world and her beings. Taking time and energy to understand oneself, and to then to manage the outcomes of this understanding is not a selfish act, but a self-full blessing that nurtures us, and hence the many others to whom our souls are deeply connected.

The more honest you can be with seeing yourself for who you are, which means not suppressing your feelings, the more tenderly honest you can be with others. You can also more clearly communicate what you really mean in a way that helps build connections and trust with another, and this can help you be precise, open, and curious about requests you have of others and how they respond to you. If you suspect that your honest message will be painful, be ready to offer empathy to the receiver. Also, couple your honest messages with clear and doable requests in the moment.

Being honest with others helps us live authentically and be more deeply connected to life, no matter how the other people around us react. Honesty, authenticity, and connection most likely communicate self- and other-acceptance, which more likely results in being listened to and understood. In summary, honesty and empathy help us to live better with ourselves and our world, and in so doing nurtures our relationships and communications so that all have a greater chance for flourishing.

Social Intelligence

"Self-absorption in all its forms kills empathy, let alone compassion. When we focus on ourselves, our world contracts as our problems and preoccupations loom large. But when we focus on others, our world expands. Our own problems drift to the periphery of the mind and so seem smaller, and we increase our capacity for connection – or compassionate action."
– Daniel Goleman

We are always with others, and always connected to them. Our social brain is predisposed to wire itself around subconscious clues we derive from others so that we resonate with them for our benefit, for theirs, for the relationship, and for the greater group. So even if we were to be in solitary confinement or alone on an island with no other living being, we are never alone, for the "other" has been wired into our brain, and hence motivates our behavior and actions, whether we are conscious of it or not.

The goal is to be more aware of how we are a social being and to have choice around that deep connection we have with others. This awareness and the use of it is part of social intelligence. Social intelligence can also be defined as:
- The ability to get along well with others, and to get them to cooperate with you for the benefit of the relationship and the greater group
- The ability to be curious about the feelings and needs of others, and with a greater awareness of and connection to others, having choice about how to interact for healthy and productive relationships.

Each is born with social intelligence (SI), though some with more than others. After birth, the environment in which each grows also influences our ability to socially interact with others at both conscious and subconscious levels. Just as with emotional intelligence, no matter what we were born with or how we were nurtured, we each can move further along the continuum of greater social intelligence, for social intelligence is not just how we interact with others, but our awareness of our actions.

Individuals can grow their SI, and so can groups. There is good reason to grow SI, for individuals and groups that are the most socially intelligent are those that:

- Deliver greater care more quickly in more ambiguous situations
- Produce positive emotions which result in higher commitment to the organization
- Improve worker performance and satisfaction
- Have less stress, burnout, and compassion fatigue
- Have the greatest leadership ability

Empathy is one hallmark awareness and skill in SI. If we can open ourselves to another's perspective, experiences, emotions, and needs, our relationships, communications, and organizations stand a greater chance for flourishing. Empathy doesn't require that we actually like the person we are with, or even feel like we want to do something for them. Empathy just asks us to slow down enough to consider the other person's feelings and needs. Any opportunity to offer empathy *grows* our ability to offer empathy, even when under trying circumstances (such as when our own needs are not being met). Practicing empathy gives us a choice, not only of when to offer empathy to one who might need it, but also in living a life surrounded by beauty. For when opening to the feelings and needs of others, we see the beauty of the interconnection that weaves our lives into all others. To live in empathy, means we are held in a web of beauty.

Reflection Questions

1. Where do you see beauty in yourself and others, and in the world. Where do you not?

2. What factors go into how, where, and when you see beauty?

3. How do you evaluate your level of self-acceptance and emotional intelligence?

4. How can this community support you in your ongoing journey in advancing your natural intelligences?

5. How important is honesty in your life? Where do you or others around you struggle to offer honest and empathetic feedback?

6. How would you change the feelings and needs list to fit you or other species?

7. How do you communicate compassionately with other species?

8. Other questions you'd like to ask yourself or others?

Nurture Nature Practices

A. Nurturing Ourselves: Go For A Beauty Walk (every day for a week)

- Before going for a walk, read the Navajo Beauty Way

In beauty I walk
With beauty before me I walk
With beauty behind me I walk
With beauty above me I walk
With beauty around me I walk
It has become beauty again
It has become beauty again

- Walk silently along a path
- If you do not want to walk, stay seated nearby in comfort
- Just be, be yourself, be yourself in beauty
- Watch your thoughts and breathe
- If thoughts go to the past, future, "to do list" or stories or thoughts, watch them, and then let them go
- Return to the present moment. Watch yourself moving through a world of beauty, inner and outer.

- When you reach the midpoint of your walk, pause, and look up. Look all around. Hold your arms stretched out. Twirl around. Touch the ground. Sit on the ground. Roll on the ground if you can. Smile. Laugh.
- Now turn around and walk silently back
- Imagine yourself to be another being you find beautiful
- What are they thinking, feeling, and doing?
- What are they moving towards, or away from so that they can live well? What are their needs?
- If thoughts go to the past, future, "to do list" or stories or thoughts, watch them, and then let them go
- Return to the present moment. Watch yourself moving through a world of beauty - inner and outer.
- After you finish your walk or sitting, read the rest of the Navajo Beauty Blessing:

Today I will walk out, today everything unnecessary will leave me,
I will be as I was before, I will have a cool breeze over my body.
I will have a light body, I will be happy forever,
nothing will hinder me.
I walk with beauty before me. I walk with beauty behind me.
I walk with beauty below me. I walk with beauty above me.
I walk with beauty around me. My words will be beautiful.

In beauty, all day long may I walk.
Through the returning seasons, may I walk.
On the trail marked with pollen may I walk.
With dew about my feet, may I walk.

With beauty before me may I walk.
With beauty behind me may I walk.
With beauty below me may I walk.
With beauty above me may I walk.
With beauty all around me may I walk.

In old age wandering on a trail of beauty, lively, may I walk.
In old age wandering on a trail of beauty, living again, may I walk.
My words will be beautiful.

"It all begins and ends in beauty" (LoraKim Joyner)

B. Deepening and Sharing Ourselves: Empathy through Other-Empathy

(For this exercise, use the Feeling/Needs Lists in the Appendices on pages 181 and 182)

1. Find someone with whom you wish to connect, and with whom you feel you have a lot in common. Ask them if they have about 15 minutes they can share with you in a listening exercise that will nurture both of you, your relationship, your work, and your organization if you share that as well.

2. Before beginning the dialog, invite them to join you, to breathe deeply for a minute. Then, if possible, to step outside and look to the ground, then to the sky, and then twirl around slowly with your arms outstretched. Smile as you come around to the original position, and then bow with hands clasped. Explain to them that this movement opens hearts and minds to connection and prepares each for the work that smiling induces satisfaction, and that bowing brings on a sense of connection and gratitude.

3. Choose one person to go first who will be the speaker. The other will be the listener. The speaker will take five minutes to describe "their perfect" world, or perhaps said another way, describe the most beautiful world they can imagine. What would it feel, look, and smell like? What would people from various demographics be doing, feeling, and thinking? What would other species be doing, feeling, and thinking? What would the landscapes and ecological systems look like? What and how are people's relationships, families, work life, and hobbies? As each person is talking, the other listens without interrupting or commenting. Set a timer so that you know when five minutes is up. At the end, the listener guesses what the other might have been feeling while they spoke, and guesses what needs are behind their description of the world. What needs are being met in this most beautiful world? What needs are important to the speaker? The speaker affirms if the guesses are not resonating with him or her, or perhaps are. When ready, switch roles and have the listener now be the speaker, repeating the guessing of feelings and needs at the end. When completed, then each should share how the exercise was for them, and how they are leaving the conversation.

If you cannot find someone to speak with, think of someone you know, imagine doing the exercise with them, listening to them and then guessing, and then you speaking and imagining what they might guess about you.

4. After completing this exercise, invite each other to breathe deeply for a minute. Then, if possible, step outside and look to the ground, then to the sky, and then twirl around slowly with your arms outstretched. Smile as you come around to the original position, and then bow with hands clasped.

5. On the following days, repeat this exercise with different people, and as the week goes by, choose people further removed and different from you. By the end of the week, consider doing this exercise with someone with whom you have had conflict or disagreement, or someone you out and out dislike.

C. Moving from Inner to Outer Work

1. Engage in a political act, such as joining a march, meeting, or community that seeks liberation from oppressive structures. As you participate, reflect back upon the inherent worth and dignity of every being. Consciously breathe in beauty of those around and breathe out your beauty within. While there, share with others something that is beautiful about them or the gathering. Ask them if they see something beautiful too and would like to share that with you.

2. Go for a walk somewhere that has litter or trash. Pick up one piece (or fill a bag) to help make the area more beautiful.

Resources

Books
- Jane Marantz Connor and Dian Killian. *Connecting Across Differences*.
- Thomas D'Ansembourgh. *Being Genuine: Stop Being Nice, Start Being Real.*
- Raj Gill et al. *NVC Toolkit for Facilitators.*
- Daniel Goleman. *Emotional Intelligence.* 2006.
- Daniel Goleman. *Social Intelligence.* 2006.
- Sura Hart. *The No-Fault Classroom.*
- Sura Hart and Victoria Kindle Hodson. *Respectful Parents, Respectful Kids: 7 Keys to Turn Family Conflict into Cooperation.*
- Lucy Leu. *Nonviolent Communication Companion Work Book.*
- Jean Morrison. *Grok it! 150 Exercises and Games.* http://wwwgroktheworld.com/grokit-nvc-facilitation-manual.
- Andrew Newberg, M.D. *Words Can Change Your Brain: 12 Conversation Strategies to Build Trust, Resolve Conflict, and Increase Intimacy.*
- Marshall Rosenberg. *Nonviolent Communication: A Language of Life.*
- Deborah Van Duesen Hungsinger. *Transforming Church Conflict.*

NVC Training Organizations, Websites, and Resources

- NVC Academy: flexible online and teleconference trainings www.nvctraining.com
- Bay NVC: regular trainings in San Francisco area, frequent trainings throughout US www.baynvc.org
- Website with lots of games/books/ideas for children: http://www.nvcworld.com
- Family camps: http://www.cnvc.org/family-camps
- Center for Nonviolent Communication: Varied trainings in US and internationally www.cnvc.org
- Information/learning: www.nvcwiki.org, www.growingcompassion.org
- Restorative Circles: http://www.restorativecircles.org/

Guide #2: Compassion, Empathy, and Other Prosocial Behaviors

To many Humans currently appear to have difficulty empathizing w/ their own species.

Those of us who...

Nurture Nature

Yours, Ours, Theirs, Earth's

Guide #2 Table of Contents

FORMAT FOR NURTURE NATURE COMMUNITY 26

READINGS
Main Reading: Prosocial Behavior: A Multispecies Perspective 27
Additional Readings 30

REFLECTIONS
Reflection Questions 36

NURTURE NATURE PRACTICES
Weekly Nurture Nature Practices 39
Other Suggested Practices 44

RESOURCES 45

Published by One Earth Conservation, www.oneearthconservation.org
info@oneearthconservation.org

Please help us to continue to provide free resources for the public, such as this guide, by giving a tax-deductible donation to One Earth Conservation at: https://www.oneearthconservation.org/donate
All proceeds go to directly to helping the people and the parrots of the world.

Thanks to Rev. Meredith Garmon and Community Unitarian Universalist Congregation (http://www.cucwp.org/) for compiling some of these materials as part of their Journey Group program.

Format for Nurture Nature Community

We speak and listen deeply with our hearts and minds, allowing each to speak without interruptions, questions, or advice (unless solicited). The facilitator will help guide us in this so we can make the deepest connections possible to ourselves, others, earth, and earth's beings.

Arriving/Warm Up

As you arrive, make a name tag and draw a picture or write a word representing a species that is meaningful or important to you. Share with one another why you cherish this animal.

Opening Words

"Accepting our kinship with all life on earth is not only solid science...in my view, it's also a soaring spiritual experience."

– Neil deGrasse Tyson

Check In

Share your name, why you are here today and where you are from. What's been happening in your life? How is it with your soul today? Pause between each sharing for 10 seconds, and have a minute of silence after all sharing)

Shared Exploration

Watch "Born to Love - Transpecies Relationships" - https://www.youtube.com/watch?v=dUPF_bzMnUY

Our Nurture Nature Practice (Discussion and Reflection)

You are invited to share a story from your own life - a relationship you have with another species (flora or fauna) that was meaningful and/or transformative, and where they or you exhibited compassion, care, empathy, or another prosocial behavior. Discuss what these stories, video and transpecies/multispecies relationships mean to you (to guide reflection - see Reflection Questions)

Our Nurture Nature Practice (Embodiment)

Guide #2: Compassion, Empathy and Other Prosocial Behaviors

Nurturing Inner and Outer Wildness with a Walk

Next Steps

What does your deepening on this theme ask of you to do? Of us together?

Confirm facilitator, location, date/time and subject of next meeting

Check Out

From everything we've shared during this time together, what overall message stands out for you?

· What gratitude and affirmation would you like someone else to know?

Closing Words

"We can't change the world for animals without changing our ideas about animals. We have to move from the idea that animals are things, tools, machines, commodities, resources here for our use to the idea that as sentient beings they have their own inherent value and dignity. (and by animals, I mean human animals as well)"

– LoraKim Joyner and Andrew Linzey

MAIN READINGS

Prosocial Behaviors: A Multispecies Perspective
Rev. Dr. LoraKim Joyner

The more we look, the more we discover prosocial behaviors in a variety of species. Here is a short list:

Cooperating	Teaching
Mourning/Burying the Dead	Protecting
Grieving	Fairness
Consoling	Justice
Empathy	Trust
Caring/Nurturing	Friendships
Parenting	Others?

We did not see these behaviors in the past, perhaps in part because we push part of ourselves away, setting up disconnection. We also allow a dualism that invites seeing one group being better than others – my tribe, my nation, my skin color, my species against all others.

One check to this "othering" and inherent tribalism, is to develop our multispecies intelligence. Multispecies intelligence is the ability to understand and use emotional intelligence, communication, and behavior across species lines for the mutual benefit of all. It requires understanding species needs, behavior, motivations, and interconnecting relations with others and their habitat. In short, we ask, what is the individual feeling and needing? We do this in part by seeking to know the motivations for the behaviors, such as understanding their subjective experience (emotions and internal processing) and needs. This means employing what is known as critical anthropomorphism: "Critical anthropomorphism refers to a perspective in the study of animal behavior that encompasses using the sentience of the observer to generate hypotheses in light of scientific knowledge of the species, its perceptual world, and ecological and evolutionary history." (Wikipedia, Cognitive Ethology)

By engaging in critical anthropomorphism, we avoid two errors on either end of the spectrum of multispecies understanding: one is to say that other species are nothing like humans (anthrocentrism), and the other is to say they are exactly like us (uncritical anthropomorphism). Critical anthropomorphism means that we imagine what it is like to be in the shoes, paws, hooves, wings, claws, feet, and skin of another, and then to check ourselves where we might have made either of the two types of errors. We put on our scientific lens, and ask, what is this individual feeling and needing? We put on our empathetic, embodied lens, and ask, what is this individual feeling and needing? We employ all the science and sensory and body resonance that is available to us, study, reflect, discuss, check our assumptions, and then ask: How might my perception of another lead to more harm than good?

A prime example of how we wrongfully see humans in multispecies community is the statement, "Humans are the only ones who _____." In terms of prosocial behavior, I have heard it said that humans are the only ones who can choose to beneficially act on another's behalf. Other animals are using instinct or subconscious automatic behavior patterns. Perhaps they are only acting thusly because of human intervention. *If ever you are tempted to say "only humans do X," or "humans have greater choice or do similar behaviors for different reasons," or if you read, "what sets humans apart from animals" become immediately suspicious of why you or others are saying that.* You ask yourself if such a phrase is to promote human exceptionalism, where humans are better than other animals. There is another kind of human exceptionalism: where humans aren't better than others because of behaviors and intent, but are actually worse. Either way we are committing multispecies errors, distancing ourselves from ourselves and others, and setting up harm to

27

Guide #2: Compassion, Empathy and Other Prosocial Behaviors

others, and inviting despair, depression, and debilitating disconnection that disempowers us.

Prosocial behaviors are shared widely throughout life and go back deep into our evolutionary history. To understand this, I believe our minds are hard wired to easily lay down neural networks for prosocial behaviors. Our prosocial behaviors connect us to other animals and to all of life. Knowing how great is our inheritance to act on another's behalf, perhaps gives us greater compulsion and choice to develop our own prosocial behaviors, towards ourselves and towards other species. It also awakens in us a world of wonder and beauty, to offset the harm and tragedy that is interwoven into existence, and into us.

To understand prosociality in others and ourselves offers hope, and tools for a world of greater flourishing for our multispecies communities. Human aspects of compassion to keep in mind:

1. Compassion is more easily elicited when we feel safe
2. Compassion feels good (impacts pleasure centers of brain, increases life span and sense of well-being)
3. Compassion is catching in a social context
4. Mindfulness increases compassion
5. We like helping the group more than ourselves
6. We evolved to help one person at a time 乙

Keeping these aspects in mind, we can grow our prosocial behaviors, towards ourselves and others of all species. We design a schedule of self-nurturing practices that allow us the greatest change to embody compassion, and we also seek to grow our empathy and understanding of others. Later in this booklet are some Nurture Nature practices, one of which is especially important for multispecies intelligence: "Multispecies Empathy." Empathy helps us grow our understanding of other beings, as do cognitive processes such as research, study, reflection, and learning. To answer the basic question that multispecies intelligence posits, "What is this individual feeling and needing?" we require understanding the being's biology, ecology, physiology, behavior, health and welfare status. We want our empathy to be informed, or "entangled" from author Lori Gruen's book *Entangled Empathy*. Empathy happens best when we are emotionally and cognitively engaged, similar to Paul Bloom's rational compassion in his book *Against Empathy*. The "Five Domains Model" helps us grow what we know about animals, utilizing the cognitive operations of our mind so that our compassionate response is based less on the errors of anthropomorphism and anthrocentrism to which we are prone. We can never remove ourselves entirely from our subconscious self-interest and bias, our internalized cultural stories, or our own emotional entanglements based on our life experiences, but we can diminish the harm that these cause. We do this by constantly reflecting upon our behavior, emotions, and thoughts, and being able to do through a supportive community, such as this Nurture Nature Community.

ADDITIONAL READINGS

Wikipedia Prosocial Behavior

Prosocial behavior, or "voluntary behavior intended to benefit another" is a social behavior that "benefit[s] other people or society as a whole, such as helping, sharing, donating, co-operating, and volunteering." Obeying the rules and conforming to socially accepted behaviors (such as stopping at a "Stop" sign or paying for groceries) are also regarded as prosocial behaviors. These actions may be motivated by empathy and by concern about the welfare and rights of others, as well as for egoistic or practical concerns, such as one's social status or reputation, hope for direct or indirect reciprocity, or adherence to one's perceived system of fairness. It may also be motivated by altruism, though the existence of pure altruism is somewhat disputed, and some have argued that this falls into philosophical rather than psychological realms of debate. Evidence suggests that prosociality is central to the well-being of social groups across a range of scales. Empathy is a strong motive in eliciting prosocial behavior, and has deep evolutionary roots.

Prosocial behavior fosters positive traits that are beneficial for children and society. Evolutionary psychologists use theories such as kin-selection theory and inclusive fitness as an explanation for why prosocial behavioral tendencies are passed down generationally, according to the evolutionary fitness displayed by those who engaged in prosocial acts. Encouraging prosocial behavior may also require decreasing or eliminating undesirable social behaviors. https://www.youtube.com/watch?v=dUPF_bzMnUY. *Same as p.25*

SOCIAL CONTRACT

Wikipedia Altruism Examples at https://en.wikipedia.org/wiki/Altruism_(biology)

Mammals
- Wolves and wild dogs bring meat back to members of the pack not present at the kill
- Mongooses support elderly, sick, or injured animals.
- Meerkats often have one standing guard to warn while the rest feed in case of predator

Guide #2: Compassion, Empathy and Other Prosocial Behaviors

attack.

- Raccoons inform conspecifics about feeding grounds by droppings left on commonly shared latrines. A similar information system has been observed to be used by common ravens.

- Male baboons threaten predators and cover the rear as the troop retreats.

- Gibbons and chimpanzees with food will, in response to a gesture, share their food with others of the group. Chimpanzees will help humans and conspecifics without any reward in return.

- Bonobos have been observed aiding injured or handicapped bonobos.

- Vampire bats commonly regurgitate blood to share with unlucky or sick roost mates that have been unable to find a meal, often forming a buddy system.

- Vervet monkeys give alarm calls to warn fellow monkeys of the presence of predators, even though in doing so they attract attention to themselves, increasing their personal chance of being attacked.

- Lemurs of all ages and of both sexes will take care of infants unrelated to them

- Dolphins support sick or injured animals, swimming under them for hours at a time and pushing them to the surface so they can breathe.

- Walruses have been seen adopting orphans who lost their parents to predators.

- African buffalo will rescue a member of the herd captured by predators. (Battle at Kruger)

Birds

- In numerous bird species, a breeding pair receives support in raising its young from other "helper" birds, including help with the feeding of its fledglings. Some will even go as far as protecting an unrelated bird's young from predators.

Fish

- *Harpagifer bispinis*, a species of fish, live in social groups in the harsh environment of the Antarctic Peninsula. If the parent guarding the nest of eggs is removed, a usually male replacement unrelated to the parents guards the nest from predators and prevents fungal growth that would kill off the brood. There is no clear benefit to the male so the act may be considered altruistic.

Invertebrates

- Some <u>termites</u> and <u>ants</u> release a sticky secretion by fatally rupturing a specialized gland. This <u>autothysis</u> altruistically aids the <u>colony</u> at the expense of the individual insect. For example, defending against invading ants by creating a <u>tar baby</u> effect. This can be attributed to the fact that ants share their <u>genes</u> with the entire <u>colony</u>, and so this behavior is evolutionarily beneficial (not necessarily for the individual ant but for the continuation of its specific genetic make-up).

- <u>Synalpheus regalis</u> is a species of eusocial marine <u>snapping shrimp</u> that lives in <u>sponges</u> in <u>coral reefs</u>. They live in colonies of about 300 individuals with one reproductive female. Other colony members defend the colony against intruders, forage, and care for the young. Eusociality in this system entails an adaptive division of labor which results in enhanced reproductive output of the breeders and inclusive fitness benefits for the nonbreeding helpers. *S. regalis* are exceptionally tolerant of <u>conspecifics</u> within their colonies due to close genetic relatedness among nest mates. <u>Allozyme</u> data reveals that <u>relatedness</u> within colonies is high, which is an indication that colonies in this species represent close kin groups. The existence of such groups is an important prerequisite of explanations of social evolution based on <u>kin selection</u>.

Protists

- An interesting example of altruism is found in the cellular <u>slime molds</u>, such as *Dictyostelium mucoroides*. These protists live as individual <u>amoebae</u> until starved, at which point they aggregate and form a multicellular fruiting body in which some cells sacrifice themselves to promote the survival of other cells in the fruiting body.

"Prosocial behavior in animals: the influence of social relationships, communication and rewards" – Animal Behavior 84(5):2012, 1085-1093
by Katherine Cronin

Overall, primates in close relationships were more likely to behave prosocially. In many species, prosociality was more likely to be shown by dominant individuals. When recipients showed interest in rewards, prosociality was less likely. A greater benefit for the recipient than the donor often inhibited prosociality. Acknowledging these trends will aid in the reconstruction of prosocial evolution.

"Familiarity affects other-regarding preferences in pet dogs" – Scientific Reports 5:2015
by Mylene Quervel-Chaumette et al.

(handwritten: 45–er5)

Dogs donate to familiar partners more often than to unfamiliar ones. Whether the donor dogs knew the recipient made a difference. Donor dogs pulled the giving tray more often for familiar dogs than for unfamiliar ones. "Dogs truly behave prosocially toward other dogs. That had never been experimentally demonstrated before. What we also found was that the degree of familiarity among the dogs further influenced this behavior. Prosocial behavior was exhibited less frequently toward unfamiliar dogs than toward familiar ones."

The Better Angels of Our Nature
by Stephen Pinker

(handwritten left margin: We live in a Time that challenges these Assertions)

Stephen Pinker discusses these causes as being responsible for the decrease in violence over the many millennia of human evolution:

Empathy *(handwritten: World-wide ?)*
Self control
Recent Biologic Evolution
Morality and Taboo (laws, childhood development, cultural expectations)
Reason

"The growing scientific evidence that we are a fundamentally empathetic species has profound and far-reaching consequences for society, and may well determine our fate as a species...The decline of violence may owe something to an expansion of empathy, but it also owes much to harder-boiled faculties like prudence, reason, fairness, self-control, norms and taboos, and conceptions of human rights.

The overall picture that has emerged from the study of the compassionate brain is that there is no empathy center with empathy neurons, but complex patterns of activation and modulation that depend on perceivers' interpretations of the traits of another person and the nature of their relationship with the person. Neediness, like cuteness, is a general elicitor of sympathy. With less easily helped individuals, a perception of shared values and other kinds of similarity makes a big difference...Empathy can be switched on and off, or thrown into reverse, by our construal of the relationship we have with a person."

32

Empathy is a "contagious emotion."

The Hidden Life of Trees: What They Feel, How They
Communicate—Discoveries from a Secret World
by Peter Wohlleben

The answer is that trees need to communicate, and electrical impulses are just one of their many means of communication. Trees also use the senses of smell and taste for communication. If a giraffe starts eating an African acacia, the tree releases a chemical into the air that signals that a threat is at hand. As the chemical drifts through the air and reaches other trees, they "smell" it and are warned of the danger. Even before the giraffe reaches them, they begin producing toxic chemicals. Insect pests are dealt with slightly differently. The saliva of leaf-eating insects can be "tasted" by the leaf being eaten. In response, the tree sends out a chemical signal that attracts predators that feed on that particular leaf-eating insect. Life in the slow lane is clearly not always dull.

But the most astonishing thing about trees is how social they are. The trees in a forest care for each other, sometimes even going so far as to nourish the stump of a felled tree for centuries after it was cut down by feeding it sugars and other nutrients, and so keeping it alive. Only some stumps are thus nourished. Perhaps they are the parents of the trees that make up the forest of today. A tree's most important means of staying connected to other trees is a "wood wide web" of soil fungi that connects vegetation in an intimate network that allows the sharing of an enormous amount of information and goods. Scientific research aimed at understanding the astonishing abilities of this partnership between fungi and plant has only just begun.

The reason trees share food and communicate is that they need each other. It takes a forest to create a microclimate suitable for tree growth and sustenance. So it's not surprising that isolated trees have far shorter lives than those living connected together in forests. Perhaps the saddest plants of all are those we have enslaved in our agricultural systems. They seem to have lost the ability to communicate, and, as Wohlleben says, are thus rendered deaf and dumb. "Perhaps farmers can learn from the forests and breed a little more wildness back into their grain and potatoes," he advocates, "so that they'll be more talkative in the future."

Guide #2: Compassion, Empathy and Other Prosocial Behaviors

Excerpt from "Mr. Cogito Reads the Newspaper"
by Herbert Zbigniew

120 soldiers were killed

the war was long
you get used to it

right next to this news
of a spectacular crime
with the killer's photo…

it's no use trying to find
120 lost men on a map
a distance too remote
hides them like a jungle

Conservation Psychology
by Susan Clayton

The likelihood of an empathic response to another varies with the perceived familiarity and similarity of the other to us, as well as with the salience of the cues about the other's state, the range of our own past emotional experiences, and the extent to which our knowledge helps us take the perspective of the other. Studies have shown higher concern for animals with anthropomorphic traits. Conflicts, resources dependency, or aversive emotional reactions may decrease empathy.

Research suggests that emotion is a particularly important predictor of sustainable behavior. Berenguer, for example, was able to increase emotions associated with empathy (e.g. sympathy, compassion, warmth) by encouraging students to "try to imagine how [a bird or tree] feels." this empathic response, in turn, was related to a greater willingness to allocate funds to an environmental protection organization and to a stronger perceived obligation to help nature.

"The Five Domains: Extending the 'Five Domains' model for animal welfare assessment to incorporate positive welfare states"
by David Mellor

Contemporary animal welfare thinking is increasingly emphasizing the promotion of positive states. There is a need for existing assessment frameworks to accommodate this shift in emphasis. This paper describes extensions to the Five Domains model, originally devised to assess welfare compromise, that facilitate consideration of positive experiences that may enhance welfare. As originally configured, the model provided a systematic method for identifying compromise in four physical/functional domains (nutrition, environment, health, behaviour) and in one mental domain that reflects the animal's overall welfare state understood in terms of its affective experiences. The specific modifications described here now facilitate additional identification in each domain of experiences animals have which may be accompanied by positive affects that would enhance welfare. It is explained why the grading scale and indices for evaluating welfare compromise necessarily differ from those for assessing welfare enhancement. Also, it is shown that the compromise and enhancement grades can be combined to provide a single informative symbol, the scaled use of which covers the range from severe welfare compromise and no enhancement to no compromise and high-level enhancement. Adapted thus, the Five Domains model facilitates systematic and structured assessment of positive as well as negative welfare-related affects, the circumstances that give rise to them and potential interactions between both types of affect, all of which extend the utility of the model. Moreover, clarification of the extended conceptual framework of the model itself contributes to the growing contextual shift in animal welfare science towards the promotion of positive states whilst continuing to minimize negative states. *(Note: see charts on the following two pages.)*

Reflection Questions

Don't treat these questions like "homework" or a list that needs to be covered in its entirety. Instead, simply pick the one question that "hooks" you most and let it lead you where you need to go. The goal of these questions is not to help you analyze what prosocial behaviors mean in the abstract, but to figure out what, if anything, the concept means for you and your daily living. So, which question is calling to you? Which one contains "your work?" You can use these questions for journaling, or to spark conversation with others. For all the readings

Physical/Functional Domains

Survival-related factors

1: Nutrition		2: Environment		3: Health	
Negative	Positive	Negative	Positive	Negative	Positive
Restricted water and food. Poor quality food	Enough water and food. Balanced and varied diet	Uncomfortable or unpleasant features of physical environment	Physical environment comfortable or pleasant	Disease, injury and/or functional impairment	Healthy, fit and/or uninjured

Situation-related factors

4: Behaviour	
Negative	Positive
Behavioural expression restricted	Able to express rewarding behaviours

Affective Experience Domains

5: Mental State

Negative Experiences			Positive Experiences		
Thirst	Breathlessness	Anger, frustration	Drinking pleasures	Vigour of good	Calmness, in control
Hunger	Pain	Boredom, helplessness	Taste pleasures	Health & fitness	Affectionate sociability
Malnutrition malaise	Debility, weakness	Loneliness, depression	Chewing pleasures	Reward	Maternally rewarded
Chilling/overheating	Nausea, sickness	Anxiety, fearfulness	Satiety	Goal-directed	Excited playfulness
Hearing discomfort	Dizziness	Panic, exhaustion	Physical comforts	Engagement	Sexually gratified

Welfare Status

Chart by David J. Mellor, published by MDPI in Animals, March 14, 2016.

Guide #2: Compassion, Empathy and Other Prosocial Behaviors

FIVE DOMAINS MODEL

PHYSICAL / FUNCTIONAL DOMAIN

NUTRITION	ENVIRONMENT	PHYSICAL HEALTH	BEHAVIOUR
Deprivation of food Deprivation of Water Malnutrition	Environmental challenge	Disease Injury	Behavioural restriction
Appropriate Nutrition Available Food	Environmental opportunity & choice	Fitness Ableness	Behavioural expression

MENTAL DOMAIN

NEGATIVE EXPERIENCES		POSITIVE EXPERIENCES	
Pain	Weakness	Saftey	Vitality
Fear	Dizziness	Reward	Calmness
Distress	Breathlessness	Goal directed	Security
Discomfort	Boredom	engagement	Contentment
Denility	Frustration	Playfulness	Affectionate
Weakness	Anger	Curiosity	companionability
Dizziness	etc...		etc...

WELFARE STATUS

Guide #2: Compassion, Empathy and Other Prosocial Behaviors

that are not explicitly multispecies, ask yourself:

    a. How is the author addressing or not addressing a multispecies perspective?

    b. How would you add to these readings to have them address a multispecies perspective?

    c. Do the readings have more meaning to you with or without a multispecies perspective?

1. What examples of prosocial behaviors have you seen in your own species, and in others? How does witnessing these behaviors impact your own behavior and thinking?

2. Does the long evolutionary history of prosociality offer you hope and tools in your own life, and in your relationships with others of all species?

3. Where do you imagine wrong doing or judge others (of any species) for not being more prosocial? (look at previous discussion guide "Evil/harm/bad"). Are some species less worthy or more blameworthy because they are less social towards their own species or others?

4. Where do you project human behavior onto other animals, perhaps misinterpreting their feelings, needs, motivation, and behavior in terms of prosociality?

5. What might you do to improve your multispecies intelligence?

6. Are you prone to, or have you seen, examples of "the arithmetic of compassion" where humans tend to have compassion for lesser numbers of individuals?

7. What drives or limits your own prosocial behaviors?

Weekly Nurture Nature Practices

A. Face Your Participation in the Goodness of the World

Part 1: Journal. Each day for 10 days, at the end of the day, take inventory in your journal:
In what ways were you blind to that which is most life-giving?
Who or what did you refuse to see?

How or when did you neglect the magnificence of interconnected living?

Part 2: Find a "spiritual buddy" and practice your confession. At least once in the middle of the 10 days and once at the end, face your own participation in the beauty and care of the world by speaking it aloud to someone else. (This may work better if your buddy is also doing this exercise and you can take turns confessing to each other.)

B. Answer Misunderstanding and Judgment with Empathy

Martin Luther King said, "Darkness cannot drive out darkness; only light can do that. Hate cannot drive out hate; only love can do that." So, this exercise asks you to try empathizing with individuals, not by judging what they do as being "good" or "bad," but by guessing their feelings, subjective experience, and needs.

Every day for 10 days, collect or recall a story of an individual (of any species) doing beneficial or prosocial behaviors. You might recall a famous person from history who committed momentous beneficial acts, or an animal you admire. You might leaf through the morning newspaper for accounts of people behaving in ways that strike you as good, helpful, or compassionate. Begin by sketching in your journal each day one thing that that individual did that struck you as "good."

Then: empathize. This is likely to be an exercise of your imagination. *Imagine* what the purported good-doer or individual was feeling and needing that produced the "beneficial" behavior? (Note: "feeling" here refers to emotions experienced, and "needing" refers to any universally shared desire, keeping in mind that "universally shared" doesn't mean "universally indulged or pursued.") Describe those feelings (which you, too, have felt) and those needs (the wants that you, too, are prone to have) that, as best you can guess, account for the behavior in question.

No matter the species, find academic or informational resources that can shed light on the behavior in terms of causes, needs, desires, evolution, and neurobiology.

Does this practice shift the way you think and act towards yourself and others?

C. Do Something!

Kindness and compassion is catching. When people observe an act of this sort, they are more likely to do the same. Whether in your personal life, or in a more public sphere, do something beyond what is normal for you. As you act, so you impact others.

D. Multispecies Empathy Journal and Reflection Exercise

It's not all bad news out there for the beings on earth. For instance, there is decreasing violence in the world writes Steven Pinker in the book, *The Better Angels of Our Nature*. One of the main reasons he cites is empathy. Empathy functions to help humans see each other's inherent worth and dignity, and then to enact society practices, expectations, and laws that curb our biological propensities. Just because we can, doesn't mean that we do!

Is it possible that we can grow empathy for other species? Yes! A study a few years ago asked students to pretend they were a bird in trouble for 15 minutes. The control group was given no directions. Those who pretended they were the bird showed increased levels of empathy and greater desire to help the environment than the control group.

Putting yourself into the shoes, fins, wings, hoofs, paws, or talons of another is a powerful meditation. It helps us see the inherent worth and dignity of others, and as such, helps us practice the Golden Rule, which is treating others as one would like others to treat oneself. If you are Unitarian Universalist, empathy practices help us embody and act intuitively out of the First Principle (inherent worth and dignity of every being).

You can do this as a longer journal exercise that incorporates science, or by simply going to the imagination step #5. You can do this as an individual or with others.

Preparation:

1. Think of an individual with whom you have a relationship. Write here what you know of the being. What is the species? Individual name? Gender? Age? Life stage (growing, juvenile, parent, etc.). Health status? If you can't think of an individual, choose a species you would like to get to know better or understand.

2. Thinking of them over a period of time, and imagining their behavior on a given day, or after watching a video or remembering past interactions, explain what you see as if you were a reporter with as little judgment or human projection as possible. In other words, don't try to interpret the behavior at this point. Write down all the behaviors you imagine they do.

3. Now guess what you imagine they are thinking and feeling. List your guesses here.

4. To help you understand what you observed, do some research on the species regarding behavior, communication, feelings, and thoughts. You may find it difficult to find information about emotions and thinking in nonhuman species (refer to references and resources). Use the "Five Domains Model" as a guide to what another individual might be needing, and also use the "Feelings" and "Needs" illustrations in the Appendices to help you list the feelings and needs of others. After doing research, did you discover any new feelings or thoughts that occurred in the individual? If so, add them to your list.

5. **Now imagine that you are the animal. Get into their paws, scales, fur, or feathers for about 15 minutes.** Pick an animal that is in your yard or along a walk or a hike. Pick a quiet place where these other beings normally inhabit. You can also watch a video or

nature documentary Watch their behavior for a while, and then imitate it. Just be them without analyzing too much why they do what they do If you cannot be in the physical space where the others occur, imagine that you are, and if you cannot see them, imagine what they have done or might be doing now, and then imitate them. Have your body move like the other beings. Do this for five – 15 minutes, watching and then gently discarding any thoughts you have. For instance, if you think of the past, future, "to do list" or stories or thoughts, watch them, and then let them go. Return to be the other species, being them without words, and in beauty. Thoughts might arise that this is a silly exercise, or that you are not a very good ant or tree, or other judgments. Each time, notice these and then return to being the animal and watch yourself moving and being in a world of beauty. Towards the end of your time with the individual, pay attention to your body, ask yourself what are they thinking, feeling, or doing? What is motivating them to act or be in the ways that they are? How is life striving to manifest itself through their actions and processes? What needs motivate them to act in the way that they do. Share your experience with another.

6. After this sharing and imaginative exercise, continue your research and exploration. Start a list of feelings and needs for this species, if you haven't already. Add new needs that you have discovered Again, use the "Five Domain's Model" and the "Feelings" and "Needs" documents in the Appendices. Try to be as complete as possible as you go through the behaviors observed or if you have the time, a normal day as this individual. How might these needs be different from another individual of the same species, or from the average needs of this species?

7. What feelings and needs arise in you when you consider the feelings and needs of this individual?

8. What have you discovered about this individual, this species, yourself, or life through this exercise? If you have discovered anything, what needs of yours or the individual does

what you have learned meet, or not meet?

9. Go back and spend time connecting to the energy of the other being by reviewing their feelings and needs, and then do the same with yourself. Allow this to be a time of being and connecting to life, without thought of requests or demands.

10. Then consider possible actions or steps you might do, or ask of others, based on this multispecies empathy exercise.

11. Share what you have learned or experienced with others and invite them into the exercise.

Other Suggested Practices

E. Read all the excerpts in the background readings and then write your own reflection of what good, beneficial, or prosocial behavior means to you from a multispecies perspective. Share your reflection, and this guide with others.

F. Invite others to attend your group's next gathering.

G. Write up a plan for your own Nurture Nature Practice that includes growing your multispecies intelligence. What do you need to do? You might consider reading resources on animal behavior and thinking (cognitive ethology) or going outside and imaging you

Guide #2: Compassion, Empathy and Other Prosocial Behaviors

are another species.

Resources

<u>Books and Articles</u>

- Marc Bekoff. *The Emotional Lives of Animals: A Leading Scientist Explores Animal Joy, Sorrow, and Empathy — and Why They Matter*. New World Library. 2008.
- Marc Bekoff and Jessica Pierce. *Wild Justice: The Moral Lives of Animals*. University of Chicago Press. 2010.
- Paul Bloom. *Against Empathy: The case for rational compassion*. Ecco. 2016.
- Frans de Waal. *The Age of Empathy: Nature's Lessons for a Kinder Society*. Broadway Books. 2010.
- Frans de Waal. *The Bonobo and the Atheist: In Search of Humanism Among the Primates*. WW Norton Company. 2013.
- Lori Guen. *Entangled Empathy: An alternative ethic for our relationships with animals*. Lantern Books. 2015.
- D.J. Mellor. "Extending the 'Five Domains' model for animal welfare assessment to incorporate positive welfare states." *Animal Welfare* 24. 2015.
- Stephen Pinker. *Better Angels of our Nature*. Penguin Book. 2012.
- Carl Sarfina. *Beyond Words. What Animals Think and Feel*. Picador Paperback. 2016.
- Robert Wright. *Nonzero*. Vintage Books. 2000.

Nov. 12

Guide #3: Awe and Wonder

Guide #3 Table of Contents

FORMAT FOR NURTURE NATURE COMMUNITY 48

READINGS:
Main Reading: Nurturing Wonder 49
Additional Readings 53

REFLECTIONS
Reflection Questions · 59

NURTURE NATURE PRACTICES
Weekly Nurture Nature Practices · 62
Other Suggested Practices · 63

RESOURCES · 64

Published by One Earth Conservation, www.oneearthconservation.org
info@oneearthconservation.org

Please help us to continue to provide free resources for the public, such as this guide, by giving a tax-deductible donation to One Earth Conservation at: https://www.oneearthconservation.org/donate
All proceeds go to directly to helping the people and the parrots of the world.

Thanks to Rev. Meredith Garmon and Community Unitarian Universalist Congregation (http://www.cucwp.org/) for compiling some of these materials as part of their Journey Group program.

Format for Nurture Nature Community

We speak and listen deeply with our hearts and minds, allowing each to speak without interruptions, questions, or advice (unless solicited). The facilitator will help guide us in this, so we can make the deepest connections possible to ourselves, others, earth, and earth's beings.

Arriving/Warm Up

As you arrive, make a name tag and draw a picture or write a word representing where you have experienced awe or wonder. Share with one another why you drew what you did.

Opening Words

"Those around you are also you – their wonder and beauty is yours, as is the whole world's. We need to own how awesome is our thinking, feeling, actions, and presence in the world. If we do not wonder at ourselves, we shut down the possibility to marvel and connect with all of life. This takes practice, and for that we gather today."

– LoraKim Joyner

Check In

Share your name, why you are here today and where you are from. If inclined, share where have you recently experienced wonder. If your group meets for a longer time, and the group is not large, share what's been happening in your life; How is it with your soul, spirit, mind, body today? (Pause between each sharing for 10 seconds, and have a minute of silence after all sharing.)

Shared Exploration

Review the Main Reading and points that you think are helpful for you and others.

Our Shared Nurture Nature Practice (Discussion and Reflection)

You are invited to share a story from your own life – a relationship you have with another species (flora or fauna) that was wondrous and awesome.

Discuss what these stories and resources in this packet mean to you (to guide reflection – see Reflection Questions)

Our Nurture Nature Practice (embodiment)

Nurturing Wonder and Inner/Outer Wildness with a Walk. Go for a short walk together, sharing with one another what is wondrous and awesome by using the phrases, "Wow, Really, Dude, I'm Good."

Next Steps

What does your deepening on this theme ask of you to do? Of us together?
Confirm facilitator, location, date/time and subject of next meeting

Check Out

From everything we've shared during this time together, what overall message stands out for you?
What gratitude and affirmation would you like someone else to know?

Closing Words

If you really experienced the awe and wonder of this earth…
"What song would come out of your mouth, what prayer, what praises, what sacred offering, what whirling dance, what religion, and what reverential gesture would you make to greet that world, every single day that you were in it?"
– Victoria Safford

MAIN READINGS

Nurturing Wonder
Rev. Dr. LoraKim Joyner

People report having three awe-inspiring experiences a week. How many do you have? Think back on this week – how many times did you drop your jaw or open your eyes in amazement? Do you wish you had more wonder in your life? Whatever you answer, there are reasons to cultivate more wonder.

To understand why we would want more wonder, let's think about why it exists at all. Where did it come from? No one is sure, but it seems that it comes from a long way back. Jane Goodall was observing her chimpanzees in Gombe when she noticed a male chimp gesturing excitedly at a beautiful waterfall. He perched on a nearby rock and gaped at the flowing torrents of water for a good 10 minutes. Goodall and her team saw such responses on several occasions. She concluded that chimps have a sense of wonder, even speculating about a nascent form of spirituality in our simian cousins.

Wonder helps us connect with that which is good. Wonder, like other emotions, evolved as a motivator to help us move towards satisfaction or benefit, and away from discomfort or harm. It balances with other emotions. A classic example of this how people react to live encounters with a bear in the wild, at least classic for those of us who have lived in Alaska where all life can be distilled down to bear stories or metaphors. Wonder draws us out to the woods in hopes of seeing a bear, and fear makes us keep our distance. Too much fear and we never go out, too much wonder and we are lunch.

Wonder helps us move towards that which is good or might be good for us. We open, we connect, and life's possibilities open before us. Wonder helps us engage with the world to live in ways that integrate the reality that beauty is ever present. And it helps us face the also true, but harsher, reality of harm, illness, death, and disappointment. Without wonder, we risk closing off to life, living shallower lives, experiencing less intimacy and vibrancy. One study showed that if you take teenagers rafting, a week later they report being more engaged and curious about the world. Wonder also lifts depression, and research has demonstrated that after experiencing wonder people have less inflammation in their bodies, as measured in their saliva. It also helps our prosocial behaviors – we become more empathetic, humble, and generous. When we have more empathy, others resonate with us better and we have improved relationships. Our self identity moves from a separate self to being part of a whole, or the whole itself. By merely writing about awe, we become kinder and more compassionate, and this can extend to other species and the biotic community as a whole.

I lead Nurture Nature workshops and retreats where we look out how we have choice in moving towards that which is good for us and others. How can we nurture human nature so that we can nurture all of nature is, I believe, an important question in this time of climate change, loss of biodiversity, and extinction. And two primary aspects of human nature we nurture is wonder and its partner, empathy.

There are many ways to nurture wonder, as Rumi wrote: "Let the beauty we are be what we do, there are hundreds of ways to kneel and kiss the ground." Let me suggest four ways that all involve slowing down. An overall methodology is this:

- Notice the small things
- Learn side by side,
- Provide resources for deeper exploration. This means learning the science and mechanics of existence.
- Make connections showing how we all are part of the web of life. Repeat, repeat, repeat this understanding of reality.

To do all of this we need to first slow down. We can then go deeper and deeper into the following four general areas where wonder can be nurtured.

The first area is to wonder out in nature. These are "wow" experiences. For example, I was leading a multigenerational bird tour once in New Mexico with one of our congregations there, and the children were out of their daily routine, and were perhaps a bit hesitant, especially Joey. His mother had a cocaine habit, and he was born addicted to cocaine and had issues with connecting and resonating with others. We had come across a field full of snow geese, bright white in the sun. Suddenly they all took to the air, their wings vibrating in the very depths of our body and ancestral knowing. The children, transformed, came alive with pure joy and connection, especially Joey, who jumped, danced, cried out, and ran to his grandparents to be close to them, to be held, to connect, to share in that wonder together.

Nature is full of unexpected and surprising events that we cannot foresee, and this is good for us. James Austin, a neurologist, encourages us to have nature experiences, because they help integrate our neurological processing and contribute to mindfulness and living in the present moment with attention and gratitude. He particularly suggests looking up, and in his writing he describes an example of what happened to me years ago.

I was out walking in Guatemala studying parrot nests, and my guide was a local Guatemalan. We weren't seeing many birds and so we began to talk. He wanted to tell me of his love of Jesus and Mary, and I put up my guard a little bit, unsure if he was proselytizing and expecting something from me. I was disconnecting and moving away. Then we came up to the forest's edge where the sun was just rising over the tree tops in a shroud of misty fog. Suddenly a loud flock of parrots burst forth from the tree canopy. Before I knew what happened, I was on my knees in the grass, weeping. I had been so startled with awe and beauty, I just fell. Afterwards I was a little embarrassed, but more than anything I had a sudden clarity and connection to humanity and the world. I knew that when people said words like Mary and Jesus, it was like when I said birds and trees. That experience was part of moving towards things spiritual, towards beauty, towards service, and towards an ease around religious differences, for I see the wonder moving beneath it all.

According to Dr. Austin, my experience was not usual. Indeed, in another study he asked students to gaze up at trees, a task shown to evoke awe. The other half (the control group) turned their backs to the trees. Afterwards the researchers approached each group of students with a questionnaire and pretended to trip and drop pens on the ground. The awe-struck group picked up 10% more pens than the control group, and also felt less entitled to receive payment for their participation in the study.

So, looking up is good for us. Look at trees, birds, the moon. Why not take a moment right now to look up at trees? Experiences of wonder in nature are "wow" experiences. As with other emotions, making the facial expressions of wonder and even acting as if you are experiencing it, helps to actually evoke it. Would you say it loudly with me now? **WOW!**

The second area in which to develop wonder is in the ordinary. Nature isn't just out there, it's everywhere, and it's in us. How do we evoke wonder for the ordinary, and move towards the banal and boring? The uncomfortable even? It's one thing to wonder at the rainbow of colors in our trees this time of year, but how do we do it when the leaves are brown and gone? Or on a train ride, reading headlines of disaster and death? Can't there be something more to wonder at than the last audacious thing a crazy politician said? Really? It takes practice to cultivate wonder in daily things, and move from saying "really" as a an exasperated, disappointed, or bored response to saying with positive amazement "really!" when encountering what at first glance appears mundane. Say it with me, would you? **"REALLY?"**

To grow wonder, slow down and ask this: How did that get to be here? Why is it here? What is it doing and thinking? How is it connected to me and the web of life? Pick something in the room you're in that is boring. Maybe pick a piece of wooden furniture. How did it get to be here? Woody trees only evolved in the late Devonian period about 360 million years ago. The appearance of trees and forests were one of the triggers for the two major extinction events in the Devonian where over 50% of the world's genera went extinct. Today there are 3 trillion trees, 400 for every human. There are more of them than us, and they caused terrible drastic climate change and extinction when they first appeared. We're not so bad, eh?

This leads us to the third area for evoking wonder and to learn about nurturing nature; that is, by seeing wonder in our own kind. If we could tap into the wonder of the miracle of our own existence, not just in babies and geniuses, what might our lives look like to see beauty in all the faces around us, for much of the time? How are we here at all? What are we thinking and feeling? How can we build bridges and go into space? Why is it that we can be kind to others, given all the challenges of life?

From my experience as a minister and conservationist, one of the biggest spiritual challenges I see is for people to see wonder in our own kind. We need to go from being bored or blaming, which can be summed up with a negative attitude of "Dude!" Instead we move to the Dude kind of attitude that is a softer, more positive and grateful "Dude!" Say it with me please and then look at those around you. **"DUDE!"**

#4?

51

Guide #3: Awe and Wonder

Those around you are also you – their wonder and beauty is yours, as is the whole world's. We need to own how awesome is our thinking, feeling, actions, and presence in the world. If we do not wonder at ourselves, we shut down the possibility to marvel and connect with all of life. This takes practice. So, let us practice together. Repeat after me, "*I'M GOOD!*"

Now, let's put it all together: *WOW! REALLY? DUDE! I'M GOOD!*

ADDITIONAL READINGS

Definitions of Awe

<u>awe</u> (n) c. 1300, *aue*, "fear, terror, great reverence," earlier *aghe*, c. 1200, from a Scandinavian source, such as Old Norse *agi* "fright;" Old High German *agiso* "fright, terror," Gothic *agis* "fear, anguish." From Proto-Indo-European *agh-es* (source also of Greek *akhos* "pain, grief"), from root *agh* "to be depressed, be afraid" (see *ail*). Current sense of "dread mixed with admiration or veneration" is due to biblical use with reference to the Supreme Being. To *stand in awe* (early 15c.) originally was simply to *stand awe*. *Awe-inspiri*ng is recorded from 1814.

<u>awestruck</u> (adj.) 1630s, "overwhelmed by reverential fear"

<u>awesome</u> (adj.) "profoundly reverential." Meaning "inspiring awe" is from 1670s; weakened colloquial sense of "impressive, very good" is recorded by 1961 and was in vogue from after c. 1980.

<u>awful</u> (adj.) c. 1300, *agheful* "worthy of respect or fear." Weakened sense "very bad" is from 1809; weakened sense of "exceedingly" is by 1818.

<u>Synonyms</u>: wonder, reverence, respect, admiration, dread, fear, esteem, astonishment, stupefaction

Definitions of Wonder

<u>wonder</u> n. something strange and surprising; a cause of surprise, astonishment, or admiration; the emotion excited by what is strange and surprising; a feeling of surprised or puzzled interest, sometimes tinged with admiration. From Old English *wundor*, "marvelous thing, miracle, object of astonishment." In Middle English it came to also mean the emotion associated with such a sight.

<u>wonder</u> v. to think or speculate curiously; to be filled with admiration, amazement, or awe; marvel (often followed by at); to doubt. From Old English *wundrian* "be astonished," also "admire; make wonderful, magnify." Sense of "entertain some doubt or curiosity" is late 13c. <u>Synonyms</u>: doubt, reverence, surprise, astonishment, amazement, bewilderment, awe, uncertainty, meditate, ponder, question, marvel, conjecture

"Do Animals Have Spiritual Experiences? Yes, They Do" by Mark Bekoff

So, what can we say about animal <u>spirituality</u>? Of course, much turns on how the word "spiritual" is defined, but for the moment let's simply consider nonmaterial, intangible, and introspective experiences as spiritual, of the sort that humans have.

Consider waterfall dances, which are a delight to witness. Sometimes a chimpanzee, usually an adult male, will dance at a waterfall with total abandon. Why? The actions are deliberate but obscure. Could it be they are a joyous response to being alive, or even an expression of the chimp's awe of <u>nature</u>? Where, after all, might human spiritual impulses originate?

<u>Jane Goodall</u> (2005. *Primate spirituality. In The Encyclopedia of Religion and Nature.* edited by B. Taylor. Thoemmes Continuum, New York. Pp. 1303-1306) wonders whether these dances are indicative of religious behavior, precursors of religious ritual. She describes a chimpanzee approaching one of these falls with slightly bristled hair, a sign of heightened arousal. "As he gets closer, and the roar of the falling water gets louder, his pace quickens, his hair becomes fully erect, and upon reaching the stream he may perform a magnificent display close to the foot of the falls. Standing upright, he sways rhythmically from foot to foot, stamping in the shallow, rushing water, picking up and hurling great rocks. Sometimes he climbs up the slender vines that hang down from the trees high above and swings out into the spray of the falling water. This 'waterfall dance' may last ten or fifteen minutes." Chimpanzees also dance at the onset of heavy rains and during violent gusts of wind. Goodall asks, "Is it not possible that these performances are stimulated by feelings akin to wonder and awe? After a waterfall display the performer may sit on a rock, his eyes following the falling water. What is it, this water?"

Goodall wonders, "If the chimpanzee could share his feelings and questions with others, might these wild elemental displays become ritualized into some form of animistic religion? Would they worship the falls, the deluge from the sky, the thunder and lightning — the gods of the elements? So all-powerful; so incomprehensible."

using humans as standard of comparison

Goodall admits that she'd <u>love</u> to get into their minds even for a few moments. It would be worth years of research to discover what animals see and feel when they look at the stars. In June 2006, Jane and I visited the Mona Foundation's chimpanzee sanctuary near <u>Girona, Spain</u>. We were told that Marco, one of the rescued chimpanzees, does a dance during thunderstorms during which he looks like he is in a trance. Perhaps numerous animals engage in these rituals, but we haven't been lucky enough to see them. Even if they are rare, they are important to note and to study.

"Animals Said to Have Spiritual Experiences" from *Discovery News*

Animals (not just people) likely have spiritual experiences, according to a prominent neurologist who has analyzed the processes of spiritual sensation for over three decades. Research suggests that spiritual experiences originate deep within primitive areas of the human brain -- areas shared by other animals with brain structures like our own. The trick, of course, lies in proving animals' experiences.

"Since only humans are capable of language that can communicate the richness of spiritual experience, it is unlikely we will ever know with certainty what an animal subjectively experiences," Kevin Nelson, a professor of neurology at the University of Kentucky, told Discovery News.

"Despite this limitation, it is still reasonable to conclude that since the most primitive areas of our brain happen to be the spiritual, then we can expect that animals are also capable of spiritual experiences," added Nelson, author of the book "The Spiritual Doorway in the Brain."

"Two Hearts" from *Leaping: Revelations and Epiphanies* by Brian Doyle

Some months ago my wife delivered twin sons one minute apart. The older is Joseph and the younger is Liam. Joseph is dark and Liam is light. Joseph is healthy and Liam is not. Joseph has a whole heart and Liam has half. This means that Liam will have two major surgeries before he is three years old. The first surgery – during which a doctor will slice open my son's chest with a razor, saw his breastbone in half. And reconstruct the flawed plumbing of his heart – is imminent.

I have read many pamphlets about Liam's problem. I have watched many doctors' hands drawing red and blue lines on pieces of white paper. They are trying to show me why

Liam's heart doesn't work properly. Blue lines are for blood that needs oxygen. Red lines are for blood that needs to be pumped out of the heart. I watch the markers in the doctors' hands. Here comes red, there goes blue. The heart is a railroad station where the trains are switched to different tracks. A normal heart switches trains flawlessly two billion times in a life; in an abnormal heart, like Liam's, the trains crash and the station crumbles to dust.

There are many nights just now when I tuck Liam and his wheezing train station under my beard in the blue hours of night and think about his Maker. I would kill the god who sentenced him to such awful pain. I would stab him in the heart like he stabbed my son. I would shove my fury in his face like a fist. But I know in my own broken heart that this same god made my magic boys, shaped their apple faces and coyote eyes, put joy in the eager suck of their mouths. So it is that my hands are not clenched in anger but clasped in confused and merry and bitter prayer.

I talk to God more than I admit. "Why did you break my boy?" I ask.
I gave you that boy, he says, and his lean brown brother, and the elfin daughter you love so.
"But you wrote death on his heart," I say.
I write death on all hearts, he says, just as I write life.

This is where our conversation always ends, and I am left holding the extraordinary awful perfect prayer of my second son, who snores like a seal, who might die tomorrow, who did not die today.

"Embraced by the Night" from *War Zone Faith:*
An Army Chaplain's Reflections from Afghanistan
by George Tyger

Darkness falls. I sit outside on a clear night looking up at the vast starlit sky. One more day down. How many more to go?

Above, the dome of the sky rounds gracefully into the dark horizon. Beyond that, mystery and wonder. Some things are too vast to fathom. To attempt to understand them ends only in misunderstanding. Other things are finite. They have a beginning. They have an end. Our time here is one of those comprehensible things. Sometimes it can seem like an eternity, but it is not. It had a beginning. It has an end.

One of the great mistakes is to confuse ultimate mystery with finite reality. We want to understand things, so we bring them down to our level. But some things can only be felt in our souls as awe and wonder.

Human beings have tried to name this Truth. We have tried to capture it in words. The great religious traditions each give us a glimpse of it. But none of these words or glimpses can describe the Holy.

We can hold the finite. We must allow the infinite to hold us. Mistaking the two leads to disappointment when the finite slips from our grasp and we are left reaching for empty air.

For a moment, I look at the stars and long to be home. I long to hold my wife and children in my arms and feel the familiar warmth of their touch. At this moment, even one day more seems too much.

Then I look again. I imagine I am not held captive by the finite days ahead, but embraced by the infinite Truth beyond. I know somehow that the same mystery and wonder that embrace me embrace my family, embrace all. In a real sense, if just for a moment, embraced by God, I am home.

Excerpt from "The Greatest Gift" from *Red Bird*
by Mary Oliver

What is the greatest gift?...

Something else – something else entirely
holds me in thrall.

That you have a life that I wonder about
more than I wonder about my own.

That you have a life – courteous, intelligent –
that I wonder about more than I wonder about my own.

That you have a soul – your own, no one else's –
that I wonder about more than I wonder about my own...

"The Art of the Commonplace"
by Wendell Berry

We have lived by the assumption that what was good for us would be good for the world. And this has been based on the even flimsier assumption that we could know with any certainty what was good even for us. We have fulfilled the danger of this by making our personal pride and greed the standard of our behavior toward the world – to the incalculable disadvantage of the world and every living thing in it. And now, perhaps very close to too late, our great error has become clear. It is not only our own creativity – our own capacity for life – that is stifled by our arrogant assumption; the creation itself is stifled.

We have been wrong. We must change our lives, so that it will be possible to live by the contrary assumption that what is good for the world will be good for us. And that requires that we make the effort to know the world and to learn what is good for it. We must learn to cooperate in its processes, and to yield to its limits. But even more important, we must learn to acknowledge that the creation is full of mystery; we will never entirely understand it. We must abandon arrogance and stand in awe. We must recover the sense of the majesty of creation, and the ability to be worshipful in its presence. For I do not doubt that it is only on the condition of humility and reverence before the world that our species will be able to remain in it.

"The Pleasures and Sorrows of Work"
by Alain de Botton

For thousands of years, it had been nature – and its supposed creator – that had had a monopoly on awe. It had been the icecaps, the deserts, the volcanoes and the glaciers that had given us a sense of finitude and limitation and had elicited a feeling in which fear and respect coagulated into a strangely pleasing feeling of humility, a feeling which the philosophers of the eighteenth century had famously termed the sublime.

But then had come a transformation to which we were still the heirs. Over the course of the nineteenth century, the dominant catalyst for that feeling of the sublime had ceased to be nature. We were now deep in the era of the technological sublime, when awe could most powerfully be invoked not by forests or icebergs but by supercomputers, rockets and particle accelerators. We were now almost exclusively amazed by ourselves.

"What If"
by Victoria Safford

What if there were a universe, a cosmos, that began in shining blackness, out of nothing, out of fire, out of a single, silent breath, and into it came billions and billions of stars, stars beyond imagining, and near one of them a world, a blue-green world so beautiful that learned clergymen could not even speak about it cogently, and brilliant scientists in trying to describe it began to sound like poets, with their physics, with their mathematics, their empirical, impressionistic musing?

What if there were a universe in which a world was born out of a smallish star, and into that world (at some point) flew red-winged blackbirds, and into it swam sperm whales, and into it came crocuses, and wind to lift the tiniest hairs on naked arms in spring when you run out to the mailbox, and into it at some point came onions, out of soil, and came Mount Everest, and also the coyote we've been seeing in the woods about a mile from here, just after sunrise in these mornings when the moon is full? (The very scent of him makes his brother, our dog, insane with fear and joy and ancient inbred memory.) Into that world came animals and elements and plants, and imagination, the mind, and the mind's eye.

If such a universe existed and you noticed it, what would you do? What song would come out of your mouth, what prayer, what praises, what sacred offering, what whirling dance, what religion, and what reverential gesture would you make to greet that world, every single day that you were in it?

Reflection Questions

Don't treat these questions like "homework" or a list that needs to be covered in its entirety. Instead, simply pick the one question that "hooks" you most and let it lead you where you need to go. The goal of these questions is not to help you analyze what wonder or awe means in the abstract, but to figure out what, if anything, the concept means for you and your daily living. So, which question is calling to you? Which one contains "your work?" You can use these questions for journaling, or to spark conversation with others. For all the readings that are not explicitly multispecies, ask yourself:

a. How is the author addressing or not addressing a multispecies perspective?

b. How would you add to these readings to have them address a multispecies perspective?

c. Do the readings have more meaning to you with or without a multispecies perspective?

1. What is an actual experience of wonder or awe that you have had in nature, or with a being? Can you explain why you had it? What were the lasting experiences of it?

2. Which species or individuals elicit awe and wonder most for you? Why? Which elicit the least? Why?

3. Have you ever noticed another species experiencing awe or wonder, or some sense of spirituality? Do you think that it happens more than you are able to observe?

4. Why do humans and other species experience awe and wonder? Is there a purpose to it, evolutionary speaking?

5. How often do you experience awe or wonder every week? Do you wish for more? Less? If so, what is your plan for accomplishing your goal?

6. For some, a sense of awe can be so overwhelming or intense, it feels like fear. How have you experienced the connections of fear and awe in your life? Can you describe a time that you experienced awe and fear together? Can you imagine such a feeling?

7. Can your moments of fear be transformed into awe?

8. What do pain, anguish, grief, and ailing (all etymologically connected with "awe") have to do with awe?

9. Do you find awe in the special – or in the ordinary? Is that where you wish you experienced awe?

10. Can awe be cultivated – your proclivity for experiencing it more often or more intensely improved? Or is it out of your control? If it can be cultivated, how?

11. Are you a collector, appreciator, seeker, integrator, or ignorer of moments of awe? Do you seek them out or just notice them when they come along? Do they seem to pass you by? Or when they do cross your path, do they slip through your fingers and evaporate into the air?

12. John Milton writes about "encounters and transcendent moments of awe that change forever how we experience life and the world." Has this been true for you? Have your moments of awe really "changed forever" how you experience life in the world? If so, how? If not, do you see that as a problem or spiritual challenge?

13. Does noticing awe require the "eyes and mind of a child?" Many religious traditions claim this to be the case. Has this been true for you?

14. Does awe require age? Is innocence or experience the best doorway into awe? How has your relationship to awe changed with time, age, and experience?

15. What's something you know now about awe that you didn't know when you were 18 years old?

16. What is the relationship between love and awe? Is it that love gives us access to something larger than ourselves? Poets talk about love as offering us the "promise of forever and eternity." Is awe a part of your intimate relationships? If not, do you wish it were?

17. When was the last time you were "wholly dissolved?" Is this what awe feels like to you?

18. Does a life without awe count? Do you believe that human beings are in some sense "created for awe?" Do we have a "responsibility to awe?"

19. For you, is it really more about "aww" than "awe?"

20. When you were young, was your sense of wonder encouraged or squashed? How is the legacy of that playing out today? How do you want to change that legacy? Or build on it?

21. Do you take the time to wonder? We make time for what matters. Does your life prove that wonder matters to you? How might you need to be more intentional about making room for wonder?

22. Which wonders are you embarrassed by? Many of us have experiences of wonder we keep secret. We worry our "rational" friends would worry about us if we told them about it. Or judge us. Is this the month you might be able to finally share it out loud?

23. What's wrong with trying to figure it out? The introduction to this packet talked about wonder and inquiry being two different things. Does that make sense to you? Have the two been more closely related in your life? What's at stake here?

24. Why have you stopped wondering? You once were a dreamer, but now you talk more about the importance of being realistic and responsible. There was a time when you couldn't wait to see how things were going to turn out, but now you are fine with how things are. This may not describe you at all. But then again maybe it does. Are you OK with that?

25. Do you believe in miracles? It's not really more complicated than that. Miracles are the biggest wonders of all. How do you define a miracle? Why is it important to you that others understand what you mean?

26. What takes the wonder out of your holidays and vacations, or formal religious or spiritual events? Do you wish for more during this time?

27. What does a different generation need to know about wonder? Why haven't you told them yet? What do you wonder about wonder? What question do you wish had been asked on this list? Why does that missing question hook you?

28. As always, if none of the above questions connect with you, identify your own.

Weekly Nurture Nature Practices

A. Share an Ordinary Wonder

What seemingly simple thing sustains your sense of reverence right now? What ordinary object or relationship reminds you of life's preciousness? What is currently helping you not take things for granted? Or even, what keeps you curious and engaged? Hopefully, this is an easy question for you. If not, figure out why and use this month to reconnect with the source of ordinary wonder that is surely right under your nose. Journal about this and/or share this with someone else.

Either way your task is straight-forward: bring in an object or story to your group that testifies to our everyday lives as a source of wonder. One more piece: be sure to also share why this wonderful thing sitting in the center of your ordinary life makes everything not feel so ordinary.

B. Who's Been Wonderful Lately?

We say it with a huge smile: "I love it when people surprise me!" The jerk at the office who, out of nowhere, is the one most kind. The nervous and cautious child of yours who unexpectedly turns brave. The self-sacrificing friend who finally stands up for herself. All of them leave us in wonder at what people are capable of – and of what we are capable of.

This assignment challenges you to find at least two "wonder folk" this month – two people who surprise you, two people who remind you why it's important to never write people off. Journal about this or share this with someone else. If you are feeling courageous, share it with the person who surprised you.

C. Take a Walk Until the World Lights Up

You might want to start early in the morning or in the evening right after dinner. You could also set aside a Saturday afternoon. Whenever you start, your one rule is that you can't stop until awe has crossed your path. In a sense, this exercise is an act of faith – faith that awe is scattered all over the place waiting for us to notice it, rather than believing that awe is this one rare thing that only shows up a precious few times in our lives.

Other Suggested Practices

D. Read all the excerpts in the background readings and then write your own reflection of what role wonder and awe have in your life. Make a plan for how you can grow your nurturing practice of awe and wonder.

E. Invite others to attend the next gathering of this group.

F. Help someone else (human or otherwise) have a wonder or awe experience by joining them in nature or sharing a marvel about another species.

Resources

Multispecies Perspectives

- Mark Bekoff. "Do Animals Have Spiritual Experiences? Yes they do." https://www.psychologytoday.com/blog/animal-emotions/200911/do-animals-have-spiritual-experiences-yes-they-do

- Jane Goodall. "Primate Spirituality." http://www.religionandnature.com/ern/sample/Goodall--PrimateSpirituality.pdf

- Kevin Nelson. *The Spiritual Doorway in the Brain: A Neurologist's Search for the God Experience.*

- Jennifer Viegas. "Animals Said to Have Spiritual Experiences" *Discovery News.* http://www.nbcnews.com/id/39574733/ns/technology_and_science-science/t/animals-said-have-spiritual-experiences/#.XCP-Hc_Yo8Y

- Wikipedia. "Animal Faith." https://en.wikipedia.org/wiki/Animal_faith

Videos

- Neil deGrasse Tyson. *The Most Outstanding Fact.* http://www.youtube.com/watch?v=9D05ej8u-gU

- Robert Fuller. TED Talk on *The Emotional Experience of Wonder.* https://www.youtube.com/watch?v=u3xzUzBp4BE

- Peter Meyer. *Holy Now.* http://www.youtube.com/watch?v=KiypaURysz4

- Mr. Rogers. *Wonderings.* http://pbskids.org/rogers/video_wondering.html

- Camille Seaman. *Photos from a Storm Chaser.* http://www.ted.com/talks/camille_seaman_photos_from_a_storm_chaser.html?utm_source=newsletter_daily&utm_campaign=daily&utm_medium=email&utm_content=im   age   2013-06-21

- Jason Silva. *Shots of Awe.* http://www.youtube.com/watch?v=Yb-OYmHVchQ http://www.youtube.com/watch?v=8QyVZrV3d3o http://www.youtube.com/user/ShotsOfAwe

63

- *Everything is amazing and nobody is happy*. http://www.dailymotion.com/video/x8m5d0_everything-is-amazing-and-nobody-i_fun
- *Murmuration*. http://www.youtube.com/watch?v=iRNqhi2ka9k
- *The Observable Universe*. http://www.youtube.com/watch?v=HiN6Ag5-DrU&nomobile=1
- *We Are All Connected - Symphony of Science*. https://www.youtube.com/watch?v=2Ky2JQq8lag
- *What can an atheist possibly celebrate?* https://www.youtube.com/watch?v=ptwEV0xhTzI

Books

- David Abram. *The Spell of the Sensuous: Perception and Language in a More-Than-Human World.*
- Diane Ackerman. *Dawn Light: Dancing with Cranes and Other Ways to Start the Day.*
- Marc Bekoff. *The Emotional Lives of Animals: A Leading Scientist Explores Animal Joy, Sorrow, and Empathy — and Why They Matter.* New World Library. 2008.
- Marc Bekoff, Pierce, Jessica. *Wild Justice: The Moral Lives of Animals.* University of Chicago Press. 2010.
- Bible. *The Book of Job.* See also, Stephen Mitchell. *The Book of Job.*
- Barbara Brown Taylor. *An Altar in the World.*
- Kelly Buleley. *The Wondering Brain: Thinking about Religion With and Beyond Cognitive Neuroscience.*
- James Carse. *Breakfast at the Victory: The Mysticism of Ordinary Experience.*
- Rachel Carson. *The Sense of Wonder.*
- Richard Dawkins. *Unweaving the Rainbow: Science, Delusion and the Appetite for Wonder.*
- Frans de Wall. *The Age of Empathy: Nature's Lessons for a Kinder Society.* Broadway Books. 2010.
- Frans de Waal. *The Bonobo and the Atheist: In Search of Humanism Among the Primates.* WW Norton Company. 2013.
- Robert C. Fuller. *Wonder: From Emotion to Spirituality.*
- Abraham Joshua Heschel. *I Asked For Wonder: A Spiritual Anthology.*
- Ann Peters. *House Hold: A Memoir of Place.*

- Chet Raymo. *When God Is Gone, Everything Is Holy: The Making of a Religious Naturalist.*
- Scott Russell Sanders. *A Private History of Awe.*
- Carl Sarfina. *Beyond Words. What Animals Think and Feel.* Picador Paperback. 2016.

Books for Children and Youth
- J. Baskwill. *Somewhere.*
- E. Carle. *Draw Me a Star.*
- Lewis Carroll. *Alice in Wonderland.*
- B. Gardner. *The Look Again…and Again and Again Book.*
- L. Hathor. *The Wonder Thing.*
- R. J. Palacio. *Wonder.*
- Chris Van Allsburg. *The Polar Express.*

Articles
- Julie Parker Amery. "This Little Life of Mine." http://www.uuworld.org/2005/03/affirmation.html
- "The History of Everything, Including You." http://hannahhartbeat.blogspot.com/2013/06/a-history-of-everything-including-you.html

Movies
- *Avatar*, a wonder-filled film about life on another planet and how one person navigates it.
- *Hubble*, follows the camera that chronicles the effort of seven astronauts aboard the Space Shuttle Atlantis to repair the Hubble Space Telescope.
- *It's a Wonderful Life*, the story of a small-town man wondering if his life really matters.
- *The Matrix*, how one person's wonder uncovers a new reality.
- *The Polar Express*, a marvelous tale about belief and wonder and the priceless gifts of Christmas.
- *Wall-E*, a possible look at our society's future and a robot who brings us back to wonder. Great for all ages.

66

Guide #4: Evil/Bad/Harm

Guide #4 Table of Contents

FORMAT FOR NURTURE NATURE COMMUNITY. 70

READINGS:
Main Reading: Evil: A Multispecies Perspective. 71
Additional Readings. 77

REFLECTIONS
Reflection Questions 83
Evil Quotations 85

NURTURE NATURE PRACTICES
Videos as Nurture Nature Practices. 87
Weekly Nurture Nature Practices. 89
Other Suggested Practices. 90

RESOURCES. 90

One Earth Conservation, 2019

© 2019 by One Earth Conservation. *Nurturing Nature Discussion and Practices: Nurture Nature, Yourself, and Your Relationships* is made available under a Creative Commons Attribution - Non-Commercial - No Derivatives 4.0 License. For more information, please visit https://creativecommons.org/licenses/.

Published by One Earth Conservation, www.oneearthconservation.org info@oneearthconservation.org

Please help us to continue to provide free resources for the public, such as this guide, by giving a tax-deductible donation to One Earth Conservation at: https://www.oneearthconservation.org/donate All proceeds go to directly to helping the people and the parrots of the world.

Thanks to Rev. Meredith Garmon and Community Unitarian Universalist Congregation (http://www.cucwp.org/) for compiling some of these materials as part of their Journey Group program.

Format for Nurture Nature Community

We speak and listen deeply with our hearts and minds, allowing each to speak without interruptions, questions, or advice (unless solicited). The facilitator will help guide us in this, so we can make the deepest connections possible to ourselves, others, earth, and earth's beings.

Arriving/Warm Up

As you arrive, make a name tag and draw a picture or write a word representing a species you really admire. Share with one another why you admire this animal.

Opening Words

"Evil is a source of moral intelligence in the sense that we need to learn from our shadow, from our dark side, in order to be good."

– John Bradsahw

Check In

Where do you experience evil or harm in your life? What's been happening in your life? How is it with your soul today? (Pause between each sharing for 10 seconds, and have a minute of silence after all sharing.)

Shared Exploration

Review the Main Reading and review points that are important for you and might be for others.

Our Shared Nurture Nature Practice (Discussion and Reflection)

What does evil/bad/harm mean to you in a multispecies perspective?
Pick something from this packet – a reading, a quote, a question, or a practice that you would like to discuss with others.

Our Nurture Nature Practice (embodiment)

Nurturing Inner and Outer Wildness with a   Walk

Next Steps

What does your deepening on this theme ask of you to do? Of us together?
Confirm facilitator, location, date/time and subject of next meeting

Check Out

From everything we've shared during this time together, what overall message stands out for you?

What gratitude and affirmation would you like someone else to know?

Closing Words

You do not have to be good. You do not have to walk on your knees for a hundred miles through the desert repenting. You only have to let the soft animal of your body love what it loves.

– Mary Oliver

MAIN READINGS

Evil: A Multispecies Perspective
Rev. Dr. LoraKim Joyner

Humans frequently categorize that which harms us as evil. Humans apply it to natural disasters, such as tornados, other species, such as snakes as described in several stories and scriptures, and to our own species. It allows us a quick and short method for categorizing that which is ultimately to be fought, dismissed, or annihilated. True, our evolution designed us to make rapid assessments and to fit experiences and objects into categories, so we could quickly defend ourselves, or move towards that which benefits us, but we have to ask today how helpful is the concept of evil. The concept of evil can lead to:

Increased violence

Decreased choice

Decreased view of others' inherent worth and dignity

Increased disconnection to other humans, including ourselves

Increased disconnection to other species, and to life

For example, evil is used to describe various terrorist attacks. Much harm and tragedy are tied up with these events, but to say they are evil circumvents necessary dialog, analysis, and understanding of the realities of terrorism, and the people behind it. It leads to categorizing entire groups of people, religions, countries, and global regions as evil, or wrong, and decreases choice as to whether we really need to go to war to defend ourselves. To describe another as evil risks seeing them as having less inherent worth and dignity, and can perpetuate violence against all manners of beings, including those of different ethnicities, religions, genders, sexual orientations, and species. Calling another evil reverts us to tribal subconscious behavior where we solidify our team's cohesion by pitting ourselves against others.

There are reasons we form tribes. One theory of human evolution involves early ape ancestors. In the trees with monkeys, apes were soon outcompeted by them. Monkeys could get to and digest immature fruits better than apes could, and the shrinking forest and broadening savannah became the apes' new territories. Their problems multiplied there. The savannah was teaming with predators, and apes needed to band together to outwit and outrun the predators, and to get enough food. But we didn't really like each other. Monkeys inherit a matriarchal social system that keeps them together. Ancient apes were less so inclined, and were relatively solitary, coming together only for mating or family behavior. We didn't really like each other or know how to be with each other, but be with each other we must, as evolution radiated us out into many hominid species. These species, too, likely competed with each other on the savannah and in the forests, perhaps accounting for the multiple humanoid species alive at the same time, but only one existing today. We evolved to be constantly checking our backs to see if another would turn on us, or would help us, and we were/are ready to do both. And when we came together in packs, we used the word or sense of "evil" to quickly insure that our pack would care for us because we belonged, and that all others were against us.

We do this not just with other humans, but with other species. Humans inherit fears of various species, including snakes, spiders, rodents, bats, and predators. It's in our genetic makeup, but though experiences and desensitization, including multispecies intelligence practices, we can moderate any genetic predispositions. We also have uncomfortable feelings around other species, because as prey we evolved to have fear and trepidation of predators. We have brain pathways ready to dislike other predators with whom we might compete, and those that might harm us. It is not surprising then that early ranchers and farmers wiped out most top predators in the USA. They feared the predators would harm their livelihood or themselves. We know now the complexities of living amongst predators, that some harm to us is probable, but our choices of what to do with predators, such as the fragile growing wolf population today, is limited if we stop at seeing them as only a being that kills.

Wolf and coyote killers are not the only ones to see evil living so close to us. All manner of beings gain our contempt and diminish our ability to see another's wonder or to choose how to deal with those we'd rather not have around, such as cockroaches, stink bugs, mice, and spiders. True, each of these can cause damage or discomfort, and we did evolve to not only have an instinctual aversion to many kinds of animals, but to also take care of ourselves, which means harming others: bacteria, plants, trees, and all kinds of insects and vertebrates that are harmed to provide us with food. To label these beings with the term "evil" perhaps exaggerates our responses, so we feel we must kill every snake and spider around our yards rather than consider choices that keep them, us, and the cycle of nature relatively intact and flourishing.

Incorporating evil into our language and conception also leads to distancing ourselves from others and from the reality of life. Instead of curiosity, possibility, and embracing reality, we shift to restrictive relationships where we see others, or even life itself, as fundamentally flawed. To see the wolf as only a possible killer, we don't see how they have family lives, personalities, and a beneficial niche in the environment. We kill them out of fear and distaste, and bury ourselves further and further into trouble, violence, and disconnection from life around us. To write off others or other species as basically just a receptacle for our fear and distrust of life, keeps us at a distance from all others, for the neural pathway of fear and distrust becomes readily accessible for whenever uncomfortable emotions are triggered by those around us. Seeing the snake not as evil, but as one beautiful one among all others can keep us in the wild garden cultivated by our multispecies community for their own flourishing.

To say that any part of life is evil instead of being a network of relationships which form us, such as the bacteria and viruses in our gut that keep us healthy and the pieces of DNA of other species that make up human DNA, is to cut ourselves from belonging on this planet and diminish our sense of identity. We are the other, and all that we are, is who they are. Humans exist because of other species. To say that any part of another is evil is to say the same about ourselves and locks us into self-loathing or distrust. We become incapable of feeling welcomed and whole on this planet, and in so doing isolate ourselves so we cannot welcome others into a network of mutuality and belonging.

Humans, though, have a difficult time really accepting that we belong as just one more animal species on earth, for if we admit that, we admit that we are caught in the same cycle of life and death as all others. We will be born, we will suffer, and we will die. We will predate, and we will be preyed upon. Our story telling minds find it a challenge to live with that truth, for there is pain and sorrow in losing those around us and considering our own suffering and demise. For example, we may tell ourselves, "Surely humans are fundamentally different than all other animals, for if we are not, then we have as little choice as others as to our ultimate fate, which is to die and be forgotten, either as individuals or as a species, in the

Presumably, Only humans aware of ultimate end

72

long line of evolution." Our existential fear of death is what some say keeps us from really moving more heartedly towards seeing other species as having worth and dignity. We do not want to die "just like any other animal" and therefore must not be "animal." And in thinking we are not animal, we push part of ourselves away, setting up disconnection. We also allow a dualism that invites seeing one group being better than others – my tribe, my nation, my skin color, my species against all others.

One check to this "othering" and inherent tribalism, is to develop our multispecies intelligence. Multispecies intelligence is the ability to understand and use emotional intelligence, communication, and behavior across species lines for the mutual benefit of all. It requires understanding species' needs, behavior, motivations, and interconnecting relations with others and their habitat. We do this in part by seeking to know the motivations for the behaviors we see in other species, such as understanding their subjective experience (emotions and internal processing) and needs. This means employing what is known as critical anthropomorphism – "Critical anthropomorphism refers to a perspective in the study of animal behavior that encompasses using the sentience of the observer to generate hypotheses in light of scientific knowledge of the species, its perceptual world, and ecological and evolutionary history." (see https://en.wikipedia.org/wiki/Critical_anthropomorphism) By engaging in critical anthropomorphism we avoid two errors on either end of the spectrum of multispecies understanding: one is to say that other species are nothing like humans (anthrocentrism), and the other is to say they are exactly like us (uncritical anthropomorphism). Critical anthropomorphism means that we imagine what it is like to be in the shoes, paws, hooves, wings, claws, feet, and skin of another species, and then to check ourselves where we might have made either of the two types of errors. We employ all the science that is available to us, study, reflect, discuss, check our assumptions, and then ask: How might my perception of another lead to more harm than good?

A prime example of how we wrongfully see humans in multispecies community is the statement, "Humans are the only ones who _____." In terms of evil, I have heard it said that humans are the only ones who murder or rape, or are capable of causing widespread extinction and climate change. If ever you are tempted to say, "only humans do X," or if you read, "what sets humans apart from animals," become immediately suspicious of why you or others are saying that. You can ask yourself if such a phrase promotes human exceptionalism? This falsely promotes the perception that death and suffering are not part of life and that it is okay to harm others without due regard and engaged discernment regarding their suffering. There is also another kind of human exceptionalism that implies that humans aren't better than others due to negative human behaviors and intentions, but are actually worse. Either way we are committing multispecies errors, distancing ourselves from ourselves and others, setting up harm to others, and inviting despair, depression, and debilitating disconnection that disempowers us.

To combat this, let us now see some examples of how harmful behavior (often considered evil) runs the gamut in life on earth. We do so to grow our multispecies intelligence and to understand how much of human behavior is in other species, *and how we often describe and think of it as different.* In the discussion section there are links to videos where you can see this behavior, and perhaps even more importantly, observe how humans describe behavior in other species. How many species can you name that commit murder of their own species? Torture? Siblicide (killing of siblings)? Infanticide? Sexual coercion and rape? Necrophilia? Deception? Please add to the partial list below.

Animals who commit:

Murder - meerkat, chimpanzees, wolves, bats, ants, spiders

Siblicide - spottted hyena, red-tailed hawks, egrets

Infanticide - leopards, bottlenose dolphins, mice, giant water bug

Sexual Coercion/Rape - sea otters, penguins, ducks, red-sided garter snake, guppies

Necrophilia - pilot whales, pigeons, lizards, frogs

Adultery/Extra-pair Copulation - gibbon, sea horses, many birds

Kidnapping - baboons, sea otters

Torture - domestic cats, orca whales

Deception - gorillas, jays, ravens

Cannibalism - Belding's ground squirrel, yellow-naped parrot, Teleost fish, spiders

(source: various Wikipedia articles, such as:

https://en.wikipedia.org/wiki/Deception_in_animals

https://en.wikipedia.org/wiki/Animal_sexual_behaviour

https://en.wikipedia.org/wiki/List_of_abnormal_behaviours_in_animals)

After describing these examples multiple times in workshops, someone inevitably says, "Yes, yes, of course we share these behaviors with others, but humans are the only ones who have a choice not to do this." What do we mean by choice in this matter? With 98% of all human neural activity being subconscious, much of what we do and why we do it never reaches the parts of our mind where there is a choice. In fact, much of our behavior is automatic or largely governed by subconscious processes, and it is only after we do something that our cortex makes us some kind of story about why we did something. As we learn more about neurobiology, we are discovering that humans have much less choice than we thought, even as little as ten years ago. At the same time that we see human behavior as largely influenced by subconscious processing, we are seeing how nonhuman behavior is governed more by subjective experience (emotions, as an example) and by choice. There is a wide spectrum of behavioral responses to how an individual of a given species reacts to certain stimuli, and this depends on genetics, physiology, experiences – in other words, nurture and nature. For instance, one wolf might share food with others in the pack, while others never will.

So, then people might say, okay I will give it to you that humans are animals and we have choices like other animals, but we are the only ones who cause suffering and harm at such great levels, and kill off so many other species and life in general. As it turns out, this too is a misperception. During the Great Dying about 2.3 billion years ago, multicellular cyanobacteria shifted earth's atmosphere by producing great amounts of oxygen, which made earth's atmosphere toxic for obligate anaerobes. In the Late Devonian extinction about 350 million years ago, when 50% of all genera went extinct, the success of plant evolution, namely trees, is considered a large contributing factor. Then in the Permian-Triassic extinction, the greatest of all extinction events when 96% of all marine life, 70% of terrestrial vertebrates, and 83% of insect genera went extinct, microbes producing hydrogen sulfur and methane are incriminated as a primary cause. Humans aren't the only ones capable of great and global harm, including climate change.

Okay, so humans are animals, have choice like others, and aren't the only ones to cause great harm. But you might still say we are evil and different because the responsibility lies with us. We have the capability to reverse our behavior at the local and global level, so as to reduce suffering and guard life. Yet we don't. I ask, do we really have that capability? Now? Soon? In time? Ever? No one knows the answer to this. Humankind is undertaking a great experiment to move from tribalism to choice, based on the inherent worth and dignity of all others. It's an audacious undertaking, and according to Stephen Pinker in *The Better Angels of Our Natures* we have made tremendous progress. There is less violence than there ever was. We have become a more peaceful species through cultural expectations, laws, and empathy. We have not become less violent because of some kind of evolutionary shift – our harmful behaviors are ever with us.

We will get out of the fix we animals are in *not* by seeing ourselves or others as fundamentally flawed, wrong, bad, or evil, but by embracing all of who we are, including our

Guide #4: Evil/Bad/Harm

capacity for harmful deeds. No matter the harmful deeds of ourselves and others, beauty does not leave us and weaves all life into a whole. If we consider ourselves evil or flawed, we will not take the steps to control our harmful behavior, because we deny it or push it away. Considering humankind or others as evil or bad means we might control others in ways that cause further harm and violence. We need to move from judging humankind, so we can love ourselves into changing our behavior to maximize good for others. If we turn from that reality of interweaving beauty and harm, we suffer from disconnection and lose the possibility to live in, cherish, and preserve beauty. So, let us now lose the words evil and bad, and tell a new story, where, sure, life and others are out to get us, but we need to get over that, for life and others are also out to help us, abundantly (see *Guide #2 – Compassion, Empathy, and Other Prosocial Behaviors*). Let us choose to build our life under that dual reality, so that in short, there is only one reality, what is and what could be.

ADDITIONAL READINGS

For each of these following excerpts, take a multispecies perspective.
Ask yourself:

- *How is this author not addressing a multispecies perspective?*
- *How would you add to these excerpts to have them address a multispecies perspective?*
- *Do the excerpts have more meaning to you with or without a multispecies perspective?*

Definition of Evil

evil (adj) Old English *yfel* (Kentish *evel*) "bad, vicious, ill, wicked," from Proto-Germanic *ubilaz* (source also of Old Saxon *ubil*, Old Frisian and Middle Dutch *evel*, Dutch *euvel*, Old High German *ubil*, German *übel*, Gothic *ubils*). In Old English, "this word is the most comprehensive adjectival expression of disapproval, dislike or disparagement" (OED). *Evil* was the word the Anglo-Saxons used where we would use *bad, cruel, unskillful, defective* (adj.), or *harm, crime, misfortune, disease* (n.). In Middle English, *bad* took the wider range of senses and *evil* began to focus on moral badness. Both words have *good* as their opposite. evil (n) Old English, "what is bad; sin, wickedness; anything that causes injury, morally or physically." The meaning "extreme moral wickedness" did not become established as the main sense of the modern word until 18c.

"Evil vs. Bad – Exposition of concept"
from *Genealogy of Morals* by Friedrich Nietzsche

"Evil" and "bad" are both opposites of "good," but of different conceptions of "good." The morality of early humans valued nobility, honor, integrity, and strength (note the etymological connection of "virtue" and "virile.") "Bad" was whatever the powerful didn't want: misery, deprivation, powerlessness. But the humble classes and their priests developed an alternative morality according to which equal rights for all was good, and oppressive use of power was evil. The first morality distinguishes good and bad; the second distinguishes good and evil.

Nietzsche called the first morality "knightly-aristocratic" or "master" morality. It comes from the early rulers and conquerors, who judged their own power, wealth, and success "good" and the poverty and wretchedness of those they ruled over "bad." Nietzsche called the second morality "priestly" or "slave" morality. It originates with priests, who despise the warrior caste and advance religious concepts to condemn their lustful power as "evil," while calling their own state of poverty and self-denial "good."

Much of what the first morality sees as "good" – nobility, strength, domination, using power to get what one wants – is "evil" by the second morality. Much of what the second morality sees as "good" – self-denial, restraint, equality, concern for the disadvantaged, respect for all – is "bad" by the first morality.

Good-Evil morality viewed opportunity as a social rather than solely individual concern: something society aimed to provide, in more-or-less equal measure, to all the people, rather than something for the strong individuals to seize. "Evil" was whatever perpetuated inequality and kept people oppressed.

Good-Evil morality, driven by resentment, is deeper, more refined, and more interesting. Good-Bad morality, imbued with casual self-confidence, took its values for granted rather than seeking to develop arguments to justify itself. For Good-Bad morality, power was self-justifying.

Nietzsche worries that Good-Evil morality renders us all mediocre. We have come to prefer safety and comfort to conquest and risk, the values of the knightly-aristocratic class. Good-Evil morality focuses on the evil of others and on the afterlife, distracting people from enjoying the present and improving themselves. (For if, as Good-Evil morality proclaims, no one is, or can be, better than anyone else, then self-improvement isn't possible.)

"Evil vs. Understanding"
by Rev. Meredith Garmon

In the late-summer and fall of 2001, I was one of five chaplain-interns at a North Carolina hospital. The morning after the 9-11 attacks, the five of us and our supervisor gathered. I said I wished I understood better what might lead someone to fly an airplane into a building. One of my colleagues asked, "You do believe in evil, don't you?" I stammered, "Sure." But I wasn't.

Labeling a person or an action "evil" doesn't explain or help to understand – doesn't tell us anything about the action or the perpetrators. In fact, in the months after the 9-11 attacks, I noticed considerable active resistance to understanding. To explain the terrorists' actions would seem too close to justifying them. Since few Americans could abide anything that might be the beginning of a justification of something so horrible, there was no tolerance for explaining. "It's evil" was all we needed to know.

Indeed, the function of calling something evil is to shut down any desire to understand it. We implicitly grasp that we cannot hate what we understand, so where there is a commitment to sustaining hatred – as was widespread after the 9-11 attacks (and continues in many quarters) – there is rejection of explanation and understanding. "Evil" has become a word we use when we're afraid of understanding – afraid of becoming unable to keep hating. Saying "it's evil" protects our cherished hatreds, for something that is evil is not to be understood, but only destroyed.

"Evil vs. Connection"
by Rev. Michael Tino

Human beings are relational creatures. We exist not as isolated individuals, but as people connected to everything and everyone around us. What happens to someone we're connected to affects us. I believe that goodness in our world is a result of connection, of real and right relationship that helps us act not as individuals, but as a community. When we see ourselves as connected to others, we are more likely to do things that make their lives better. I believe that evil happens in our world when we break those connections – or refuse to form them in the first place. When we separate ourselves from others, we are more likely to do things that affect them badly.

Guide #4: Evil/Bad/Harm

"Evil vs. Nonviolence"
by Martin Luther King, Jr.

The ultimate weakness of violence is that it is a descending spiral, begetting the very thing it seeks to destroy. Instead of diminishing evil, it multiplies it.

"Evil vs. Cooperative Orientation"
by Rev. Meredith Garmon

According to the Diagnostic and Statistical Manual of Mental Disorders, the standard reference work in the mental health field, sociopathy is a pervasive pattern of disregard for and violation of the rights of others, as indicated by any three or more of the following seven characteristics:

- failure to conform to social norms with respect to lawful behaviors as indicated by repeatedly performing acts that are grounds for arrest;
- deceitfulness, as indicated by repeated lying, use of aliases, or conning others for personal profit or pleasure;
- impulsivity or failure to plan ahead;
- irritability and aggressiveness, as indicated by repeated physical fights or assaults;
- reckless disregard for safety of self or others;
- consistent irresponsibility, as indicated by repeated failure to sustain steady work or honor financial obligations;
- lack of remorse, as indicated by being indifferent to or rationalizing having hurt, mistreated, or stolen from another.

Sociopaths can feel the basic emotions – such as anger, fear, sadness, disgust, surprise, joy, acceptance, and anticipation – but cannot feel what are called the social emotions – love, guilt, shame, and remorse. The social emotions orient us toward cooperation – but cooperative systems also create spaces for noncooperator "free riders."

Sociopathy is an evolutionary strategy – there's a niche for the sociopath in the ecology of human society. Cooperation is a difficult business. In being cooperative, we are at risk of being taken advantage of, suckered, conned, exploited. Proto-humans and humans through many ages have slowly developed ways to provide protections to safely cooperate. Setting up a police force and a legal system establishes outside enforcement that allows us to make contracts with some reassurance that we aren't being suckered; there's a system to enforce compliance. As our cooperation grew more extensive and elaborate, we inevitably created space for the free riders, the "cheaters on the social contract."

In human evolutionary history, it turns out that about 2 percent of us will find noncooperation a viable strategy for staying alive and producing offspring. Around 2 percent, in other words, is the carrying capacity of the "cheater" niche in our social ecology. If the number of cheaters falls to much less than 2 percent, then the rest of us get very trusting and naïve, and we become a population ripe for "con men" to run roughshod over our trusting ways. If the number of cheaters gets much higher than 2 percent, the rest of us put energy into protecting ourselves from scams and catching and prosecuting criminals. Then the benefit-to-risk balance doesn't favor noncooperation so much, and the number drops again.

Thus, the human genome produces, at a 2 percent rate, people genetically unable to empathize. It does so because that's the equilibrium point at which sociopathy is a successful strategy for staying alive and having offspring.

"Evil vs. Introspection of Our Destruction"
by Rev. Peggy Clarke

A few years ago, we got word that 330 trees were being torn down so that a new shopping center could be erected. In addition to killing the trees, clearing these 18 acres would displace dozens of species of animals and migrating birds looking for a place to rest. Land use is the second leading cause of climate change and much of it is done in tiny corners like the one in Dobbs Ferry, altering the balance between the natural elements required for life and the consumer drive. Our congregation organized an interfaith *Blessing of the Trees* to increase awareness and appreciation for the ancient life about to come to an unnecessary end. Even with Town Board members in attendance, there was nothing we could do to stop the oncoming destruction.

So, I called the developer. In an odd coincidence, this is a man I know. He's my sister's next door neighbor. His family and hers are both good neighbors and good friends. He and his wife once very generously cared for my toddler, so I could attend my nephew's high school graduation. My experience and history would tell me Chris Lynch is a good man.

That my son and his play together, that we've celebrate family milestones together, made our conversation more awkward than I'd have hoped. We tried to be polite while clearly standing on opposite sides of this heated issue. I begged him to value Earth, to see the life he was killing. He got angry at the selfishness of wanting him to abandon a project that would support his family. He argued that Southern Westchester is overbuilt and the perfect place for "development." I argued that death and destruction were never perfectly located.

Once it became clear we (and Earth) had lost, I stood at the nearby stream watching the chipmunks burying acorns to get them through the winter, knowing that the land would be torn apart, that their hard work would be destroyed, that they were likely to starve. I mourned for the deer that had found respite there, for the groundhogs who created many places for hiding and sleeping and playing. And I marveled at the centuries and intentionality it had taken those trees to grow and the speed and absent-mindedness with which we were about to take them down.

When I ask myself about evil, this is the story that comes to mind. Not Nazi Germany or slave-owners or child abusers, although those make sense as well. For me, it's the story of this good man doing a terrible thing with a clear mind. It's his lack of introspection concerning his livelihood and the destruction that creates. Evil is never as clear, never as apparent as I wish it was. I confront it, experience it, even know it in myself. I have since watched Chris in front of his magnificent house playing with his four kids. Evil isn't wearing a red cape, lurking behind a wall waiting to pounce. It's woven into our lives, informing us, guiding us, inspiring selfishness and blinding us to the world around us. I want it to be otherwise, I want it to be entirely Separate and Different. But, of course, life is more complicated than that. Always.

"Evil vs. Self"
by Aleksandr Solzhenitsyn

If only there were evil people somewhere insidiously committing evil deeds, and it were necessary only to separate them from the rest of us and destroy them. But the line dividing good and evil cuts through the heart of every human being. And who is willing to destroy a piece of his own heart?

"Neither Oppose Nor Support"
from *Civil Disobedience* by Henry David Thoreau

It is not a man's duty, as a matter of course, to devote himself to the eradication of any, even the most enormous wrong; he may still properly have other concerns to engage him; but it is his duty, at least, to wash his hands of it, and, if he gives it no thought longer, not to give it practically his support. If I devote myself to other pursuits and contemplations, I must first see, at least, that I do not pursue them sitting upon another man's shoulders. I must get off him first, that he may pursue his contemplations too.

Reflection Questions

Don't treat these questions like "homework" or a list that needs to be covered in its entirety. Instead, simply pick the one question that "hooks" you most and let it lead you where you need to go. The goal of these questions is not to help you analyze what evil means in the abstract, but to figure out what, if anything, the concept means for you and your daily living. So, which question is calling to you? Which one contains "your work?" You can use these questions for journaling, or to spark conversation with others. For all the readings that are not explicitly multispecies, ask yourself:

*   a. How is the author addressing or not addressing a multispecies perspective?*

*   b. How would you add to these readings to have them address a multispecies perspective?*

*   c. Do the readings have more meaning to you with or without a multispecies perspective?*

1. Do you feel that some species, or some individuals of some species are fundamentally "bad" or "evil?" Why is that? How does thinking of them in that way potentially help you and others? Potentially harm you or others?

2. What kind of harmful behavior is the most difficult for you to experience or contemplate in individuals in either human or other species? Why is that?

3. What kind of "errors" are you prone to: anthrocentrism or uncritical anthropomorphism? How might you use what you have read and reflected upon here to decrease your chance of making these false or weak assumptions? What might a multispecies intelligence or critical anthropomorphic practice or process look like for you?

4. What kinds of words are used to describe harmful/bad/evil behavior in humans and in other species? In what ways do we describe nonhuman animal behavior differently than human animal behavior? For instance, in nonhumans animals we say "extra-pair coupling" and in human animals we say "adultery." How can the language we use harm, or help?

5. Regarding "Evil vs. Understanding," have you found the use of the concept evil to be a thought-stopper – putting a halt to inquiry, learning, and understanding?

6. The concept of evil may be a device to allow hatred to be sustained. Is there ever a legitimate reason for sustaining hatred?

7. Michael Tino says "goodness in our world is a result of connection, …evil happens in our world when we break those connections." In what ways have you experienced this?

8. Martin Luther King calls for a nonviolent response to evil. Is nonviolence always the best approach?

9. Are sociopaths evil if they can't help being sociopaths? If we found a way to "cure" sociopathy and the condition were eradicated, what would our world look like? Would that be a good thing?

10. Peggy Clarke points to a connection between evil and "lack of introspection concerning" the destruction our actions wreak. Do you think as much as you wish you did about the destruction caused by your choices? (Using fossil fuels? Buying food, clothing, or other products which could not be sustainably provided to everyone?) Do you feel guilty? Is there an alternative to guilt?

11. Have you ever encountered personally something or someone who you experienced as evil? Or have you experienced someone you believe to be good acting in what seems an "evil" way? What did that feel like? How did your body react? Your mind? Did it affect your relationship/choices?

12. "We are all mixtures of virtue and depravity, capable of extraordinary horrors and extraordinary heroism" (David Brooks). Is it true that we are all capable of extraordinary horrors? How do you feel about that? How does it affect your relationships with others? Your outlook on life?

13. "The line dividing good and evil cuts through the heart of every human being. And who is willing to destroy a piece of his own heart?" (Aleksandr Solzhenitsyn) What does this mean to you? Is it true? Does resisting evil destroy a piece of our own heart? Does

Guide #4: Evil/Bad/Harm

Solzhenitsyn's perspective imply that we cannot reduce evil? Or, if we can reduce it, what does this perspective say about how to do so?

Evil Quotations

For each of these following quotes, take a multispecies perspective. Ask yourself:
- *How is this author not addressing a multispecies perspective?*
- *How would you add to these quotes to have them address a multispecies perspective?*
- *Do the quotes have more meaning to you with or without a multispecies perspective?*

"There is some good in the worst of us and some evil in the best of us. When we discover this, we are less prone to hate our enemies." – Martin Luther King, Jr.

"The only thing necessary for the triumph of evil is for good men to do nothing." – Edmund Burke

"The world is a dangerous place to live; not because of the people who are evil, but because of the people who don't do anything about it." – Albert Einstein

"Inside each of us, there is the seed of both good and evil. It's a constant struggle as to which one will win. And one cannot exist without the other." – Eric Burdon

"Many of our choices are between good and evil. The choices we make, however, determine to a large extent our happiness or our unhappiness, because we have to live with the consequences of our choices." – James E. Faust

"The evil that is in the world almost always comes of ignorance, and good intentions may do as much harm as malevolence if they lack understanding." – Albert Camus

"If money helps a man to do good to others, it is of some value; but if not, it is simply a mass of evil, and the sooner it is got rid of, the better." – Swami Vivekananda

"The lack of money is the root of all evil." – Mark Twain

"Idle hands are the devil's workshop." – Proverbs

"Far from idleness being the root of all evil, it is rather the only true good." – Soren Kierkegaard

"Since boredom advances and boredom is the root of all evil, no wonder, then, that the world goes backwards, that evil spreads. This can be traced back to the very beginning of the world. The gods were bored; therefore, they created human beings." – Soren Kierkegaard

"The belief that there is only one truth, and that oneself is in possession of it, is the root of all evil in the world." – Max Born

"Goodness is something that makes us serene and content; it is magnificent. Those who are not good are evil." – Bhumibol Adulyadej

"The whole course of human history may depend on a change of heart in one solitary and even humble individual – for it is in the solitary mind and soul of the individual that the battle between good and evil is waged and ultimately won or lost." – M. Scott Peck

"I'm not a pretty princess, and I'm aware of that, so I like music that is really intense, really bold, and characters that in a way almost have a dark side and are kind of evil because, for me, that's when I feel my strongest and fiercest, when I'm not necessarily the good girl." – Ashley Wagner

"Each of us has a vision of good and of evil. We have to encourage people to move towards what they think is good... Everyone has his own idea of good and evil and must choose to follow the good and fight evil as he conceives them. That would be enough to make the world a better place." – Pope Francis

"We know that segregation is evil. We know that the sickest children should not go to the worst hospitals. No, I refuse to pretend the problem is insufficient knowledge. We lack the theological will to do it." – Jonathan Kozol

"Evil is a source of moral intelligence in the sense that we need to learn from our shadow, from our dark side, in order to be good." – John Bradshaw

"Evil is a miscellaneous collection of nasty things that nasty people do." – Richard Dawkins

"It is your own mind, not your enemy or foe, that lures you to evil ways." – Buddha

"Evil is knowing better, but willingly doing worse." – Philip Zimbardo

"No man chooses evil because it is evil; he only mistakes it for happiness, the good he seeks." – Mary Wollstonecraft

"Evil is relative – and what I mean by that is that our villains are as complex, as deep and as compelling as any of our heroes. Every antagonist in the DC Universe has a unique darkness, desire and drive. And the reason for being of 'Forever Evil' is to explore that darkness." – Geoff Johns

"Man is the cruelest animal." – Friedrich Nietzsche

"Animals don't behave like men," he said. "If they have to fight, they fight; and if they have to kill they kill. But they don't sit down and set their wits to work to devise ways of spoiling other creatures' lives and hurting them. They have dignity and animality." – Richard Adams, *Watership Down*

"It is a fact that cannot be denied: the wickedness of others becomes our own wickedness because it kindles something evil in our own hearts." – Carl Jung

"We are all mixtures of virtue and depravity, capable of extraordinary horrors and extraordinary heroism." – David Brooks

Videos as Nurture Nature Practices

1. *Watch each of the videos listed below and put yourself in the place of the animals. What are they thinking, feeling, and needing? What motivates them?*
2. *As you watch, what are you thinking, feeling, and needing? Do these videos make you feel uncomfortable? Why?*
3. *What do the narrators' comments reveal about how humans perceive "bad" behavior in other species? In human species?*

4. *Did any of these behaviors come as a surprise to you?*

5. *Does watching these videos inspire any requests you might make of yourself or others to change your thoughts or behaviors? Do they suggest possible actions in which you might engage?*

(Trigger Warning: These videos show animals performing behaviors that might be uncomfortable for you to watch)

Deception: Chimpanzee mother sneaks tools away from son

https://www.youtube.com/watch?v=jealP0egJ9k&t=2s

Kidnapping: Hamadryas *baboons* kidnap a puppy from her family

https://www.youtube.com/watch?v=U2lSZPTa3ho

Sexual Coercion/Rape:

Fur seals attack king penguins

https://www.youtube.com/watch?v=ABM8RTVYaVw

Sea otters

https://www.youtube.com/watch?v=jGeXr18M6ew

Extra-pair coupling/switching partners/adultery:

Male penguin fights to remove intruder that female accepted as new mate

https://www.youtube.com/watch?v=Jupr_hLO9BQ

Torture: Domestic cat playing with mouse

https://www.youtube.com/watch?v=-I5UBUBrCJ8

Siblicide: Red-tailed hawk chick attacks sibling

https://www.youtube.com/watch?v=HGJqeN9oags&t=1s

Various videos and commentary that reveal what people can think of "bad behavior"

https://www.quora.com/Are-there-such-things-as-evil-animals-If-so-which-animals-are-evil

Weekly Nurture Nature Practices

A. Face Your Participation in the Harm of the World

Part 1: Journal. Each day for 10 days, at the end of the day, take inventory in your journal:
In what ways were you blind to that which is most life-giving?
Who or what did you refuse to see?
How or when did you neglect the magnificence of interconnected living?
Part 2: Find a "spiritual buddy" and practice your confession. At least once in the middle of the 10 days and once at the end, face your own participation in the sadness of the world by speaking it aloud to someone else. (This may work better if your buddy is also doing this exercise and you can take turns confessing to each other.)

B. Answer Evil with Empathy

Martin Luther King said, "Darkness cannot drive out darkness; only light can do that. Hate cannot drive out hate; only love can do that." So, this exercise asks you to try empathizing with individuals who do things that seem evil/bad/harmful to you.

Every day for 10 days, collect or recall a story of an individual (of any species) doing evil or harm. You might recall an infamous person from history who committed atrocities, or an animal you fear or that disgusts you. You might leaf through the morning newspaper for accounts of people behaving in ways that strike you as evil, or view the suggested videos. Or google "evil acts." Begin by writing or sketching in your journal each day one thing that individual did that struck you as evil or bad.

Then: empathize. This is likely to be an exercise of your imagination. *Imagine* what the purported evil-doer or bad individual was feeling and needing that produced the "evil" behavior. (Note: "feeling" here refers to emotions experienced, and "needing" refers to any universally shared desire, keeping in mind that "universally shared" doesn't mean "universally indulged or pursued.") Describe those feelings (which you, too, have felt) and those needs (the wants that you, too, are prone to have) that, as best you can guess, account for the behavior in question.

No matter the species, find academic or informational resources that can shed light on the behavior in terms of causes, needs, desires, evolution, and neurobiology.

Does this practice shift the way you think and act towards yourself and others?

C. Do Something!

Edmund Burke said, "The only thing necessary for the triumph of evil is for good people to do nothing." So, find a way this month to combat evil or harm. Whether in your personal life, or in a more public sphere, do something beyond what is normal for you – something that lessens the impact of an "evil" in the world.

Other Suggested Practices

D. Read all the excerpts in the background readings and then write your own reflection of what evil, harm, or bad means from a multispecies perspective. Share your reflection, and this Guide, with others.

E. Invite others to attend the next gathering of this group.

F. Read the quotes and then write your own quote on the topic. Share this with others.

G. Write up a plan for your own Nurture Nature Practice that includes growing your multispecies intelligence. What do you need to do? You might consider reading resources on animal behavior and thinking (a.k.a. cognitive ethology) or going outside and imaging you are another species.

Resources

<u>Books</u>
- Marc Bekoff and Jessica Pierce. *Wild Justice: The Moral Lives of Animals*. University of Chicago Press. 2010.
- Frans de Waal. The *Bonobo and the Atheist: In Search of Humanism Among the Primates*. WW Norton Company. 2013.
- Stephen Pinker. *Better Angels of our Nature*. Penguin Book. 2012.
- Robert Wright. *Nonzero*. Vintage Books. 2000.

Guide #4: Evil/Bad/Harm

Guide #5: Birding to Nurture Life

Nurture
Nature
Yours, Ours, Theirs, Earth's

Guide #5 Table of Contents

FORMAT FOR NURTURE NATURE COMMUNITY 94

READINGS:
Main Reading: Birding for Life 95

REFLECTIONS
Reflection Questions 105

NURTURE NATURE PRACTICES
Weekly Nurture Nature Practices ·106
Other Suggested Practices ·109

RESOURCES · 109

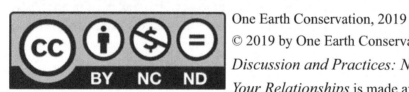
Published by One Earth Conservation, www.oneearthconservation.org
info@oneearthconservation.org

Please help us to continue to provide free resources for the public, such as this guide, by giving a tax-deductible donation to One Earth Conservation at: https://www.oneearthconservation.org/donate
All proceeds go to directly to helping the people and the parrots of the world.

Thanks to Rev. Meredith Garmon and Community Unitarian Universalist Congregation (http://www.cucwp.org/) for compiling some of these materials as part of their Journey Group program.

Format for Nurture Nature Community

We speak and listen deeply with our hearts and minds, allowing each to speak without interruptions, questions, or advice (unless solicited). The facilitator will help guide us in this so we can make the deepest connections possible to ourselves, others, earth, and earth's beings.

Before you Meet

This gathering takes place all outdoors if weather permits. Chose a location where birds can be seen and go for a bird walk. Invite someone who knows some of the local birds. Also invite people to bring binoculars and a bird guide. Alternatively, you can meet indoors, and then step outside wherever you are and look for birds.

Arriving/Warm Up

As you arrive, look around you and take in the vision of the people gathered, the trees and plants, the birds, and other life forms. Breathe deeply. If you are meeting indoors, go to a window or step outside for a few minutes and look around and up.

Opening Words

They who bind to themselves a joy
Do the winged life destroy
But they who kiss the joy as it flies
Life in eternity's sunrise
– William Blake (adapted)

Check In

Share your name and where you are from. What brings you here today? What are one of your favorite birds? (Pause between each sharing for 10 seconds, and have a minute of silence after all sharing.)

Shared Exploration

Read this guide before arriving for the bird walk.
Review the main reading and bring up any points that are helpful for you or might be for others.

Our Nurture Nature Practice (Discussion and Reflection)

Share any thoughts you have about the Reflection Questions in this guide.

Discuss what you have read in this guide.

Our Nurture Nature Practice (Embodiment)

If you aren't already outdoors, go for a walk, looking all around for birds and other life. Set aside some part of the walk for silence.

Next Steps

What does your deepening on this theme ask of you to do? Of us together?

Confirm facilitator, location, date/time and subject of next meeting

Check Out

From everything we've shared during this time together, what overall message stands out for you?

What gratitude and affirmation would you like someone else to know?

Closing Words

I once asked a bird
"How is it that you fly
in the gravity of darkness?"
She responded,
"Love lifts me."
– Hafiz

MAIN READINGS

Birding for Life
Rev. Dr. LoraKim Joyner

<u>Birding Enhances Our Spiritual Intelligence: Being the Beautiful All</u>

Spiritual Intelligence is the ability to transcend individual ego concerns and perspectives by connecting to that which is greater than the self, which fosters wisdom, acceptance, compassion, presence, and mindfulness. Our natural abilities of emotional, social, multispecies, and ecological intelligences are also about connecting to something bigger than ourselves and nurturing a greater sense of compassion, so they too contribute to Spiritual Intelligence (SI).

The goal with SI is to intentionally loosen the sense of self and increase our conscious and subconscious knowing that we are other bodies, all bodies, small and large, each and all. Having empathy for yourself, another human, other species, and the ecological web of relationships builds upon each, so that you can enter the realm of being not just one with the all, but all. You/I/she/he/it/we/they are not separate from others or the all of life, but are simply one organ, one cell, or one grain of sand in existence that makes up reality.

Mindfulness is one spiritual practice to grow SI. By bringing our awareness to the present moment, we still our inner chatter and our minds and emotions integrate in ways that bring health, choice, and compassion. Watching birds is such a mindfulness practice. One way that it serves as such is by focusing our cognitive function when identifying a bird. This keeps us in the present moment by looking at the bird and taking in its behavior, sounds, habitat, and the time of year. Many senses and cognitive functions simultaneously engage as the bird keeps our attention in the here and now. We can also let go of our reasoning process a bit and just "be the bird." This, too, is a cognitive function, but also engages the body's limbic system for greater engagement and integration of our neural processes.

We can also raise our awareness of what others are experiencing, as well as augment our empathetic abilities, by engaging in scenarios where we imagine we are the bird. Empathy is the ability to understand the emotions of ourselves and of others and is a primary component of emotional, social, and multispecies intelligence. This is helpful for us and for the birds. In one research study, Jaime Berenguer encouraged students to try to imagine how a bird feels. This exercise resulted in an increase of emotions associated with empathy, a greater willingness to spend money on environmental protection, and an enhanced perceived obligation to help nature. In another study humans were tested for tough-mindedness. A lower tough-minded score is associated with a higher degree of empathy. These humans interacted with parrot chicks raised in captivity. Greater tough-mindedness in the humans correlated with greater stress in the chicks.

Jim Austin, Zen practitioner, bird watcher, neural scientist, and author, suggests another way in which being with birds grows our awareness and, in the Zen tradition, can lead to moments of enlightenment where we let go of our daily ego concerns and feel a profound sense of connection with the All. Zen lore is full of such stories:

The disciple was always complaining to his master,
"You are hiding the final secret of Zen from me."
And he would not accept the master's denials.
One day they were walking in the hills when they heard birds calling and
singing.
"Did you hear the bird sing?" said the master.
"Yes," said the disciple.
"Well, now you know that I have hidden nothing from you."
"Yes."

Here the disciple is saying yes to life after hearing a bird call. What Buddhists have known for years we can now describe scientifically. "By regularly practicing both concentrative and openly receptive styles of meditation in ways that minimize our Self-centeredness," we can cultivate "sensitive awareness that has instant, effortless access to ...deep, global processing functions." These functions open the way not just for peak experiences of awareness and losing the Self, but also build a way for sustained awareness that operates at very deep and integrated levels in our minds.

Dr. Austin was explaining this to me one time on a bird walk and I told him about how I had a flash of opening and a sense of oneness after seeing a parrot flock burst out of the trees. He asked me if I was looking up and I answered "Yes." "What direction were you looking?" "To the right," I replied. "Were there sounds," he asked? "Yes, the birds were quite loud." He then told me that often when others speak of increased awareness, it most often comes when looking up and to the right, and often with sounds involved. I had always wondered what had happened on that morning and what had triggered the insight I gained. Was it God? Grace? Luck? Neural integration? Mother Earth telling me something? I believe it was all of this, as well as my human brain that was wired for such knowing, and for responding to a practice that can light up our lives with joy and hope.

Birding, and any mindfulness practices are not just for ourselves, though they seem to be at a superficial review. The story of Lazy An points to a different understanding. Lazy An was a monk that appeared do nothing all day but sit under a blossom tree and smile. The villagers thought he was crazy or lazy. But what they didn't notice was his joy in seeing the trees slowly blossom around him and birds alight on his shoulders. So great was his joy that he became a great leader of monks, for as others found through his example permission to be happy and to follow their childhood dreams, they also found that they had an incredible source of energy to care for others.

Birding Enhances our Multispecies Intelligence: Being the Beautiful Other

We can augment how birding helps others by focusing not just on mindfulness, but on others. We do this because humans are prone to judge others as being different, wrong, or of less worth than us. One check to this "othering" and inherent tribalism, is to develop our multispecies intelligence. Multispecies intelligence is the ability to understand and use emotional intelligence, communication, and behavior across species lines for the mutual benefit of all. It requires understanding species needs, behavior, motivations, and interconnecting relations with others and their habitat. We do this in part by seeking to know the motivations for the behaviors, such as understanding their subjective experience (emotions and internal processing) and needs. This means employing what is known as critical anthropomorphism: "Critical anthropomorphism refers to a perspective in the study of animal behavior that encompasses using the sentience of the observer to generate hypotheses in light of scientific knowledge of the species, its perceptual world, and ecological and evolutionary history." By engaging in critical anthropomorphism we avoid two errors on either end of the spectrum of multispecies understanding: one is to say that other species are nothing like humans (anthrocentrism), and the other is to say they are exactly like us (uncritical anthropomorphism). Critical anthropomorphism means that we imagine what it is like to be in the shoes, paws, hooves, wings, claws, feet, and skin of another species, and then to check ourselves where we might have made either of the two types of errors. We put on our scientific lens, and ask, what is this individual feeling and needing? We put on our empathetic, embodied lens, and ask, what is this individual feeling and needing? We employ all the science and sensory and body resonance that is available to us – study, reflect, discuss, check our assumptions – and then ask: How might my perception of another lead to more harm than good?

A prime example of how we wrongfully see humans in multispecies community is the statement, "Humans are the only ones who _____." In terms of prosocial behavior, I have heard it said that humans are the only ones who can choose to beneficially act on another's behalf. Other animals are using instinct or subconscious automatic behavior patterns. Perhaps they are only acting thusly because of human intervention. If ever you are tempted to say, "only humans do X," or "humans have greater choice or do similar behaviors for different reasons," or if you read, "what sets humans apart from animals," become immediately suspicious of why you or others are saying that. Ask yourself if such a phrase is

97

being used to promote human exceptionalism, where humans are better than other animals. There is another kind of human exceptionalism where humans aren't better than others because of behaviors and intentions, but are actually worse. Either way we are committing multispecies errors, distancing ourselves from ourselves and others, setting up harm to others, and inviting despair, depression, and debilitating disconnection that disempowers us.

While watching birds, then, keep in mind the errors to which we are prone. We "be the bird" by letting go of reason, yes, but we also engage our critical thinking to understand the thinking, emotions, motivations, and behavior of the bird. We continually ask ourselves how we might be projecting our understanding of humans onto the bird. We check ourselves by discussing our observations with others, and by researching bird ecology and behavior and adapting our interpretation of what we see. We can apply our improved understanding to what the needs are of birds are in our area, and we can respond with greater care and activism to improve their lives, such as planting trees and shrubs that offer food, nesting, and protection for them.

Birding Enhances out Ecological Intelligence: Being in Beautiful Relationship with Life

"Ecological intelligence is not speech. It is an act. It is an act of weaving and unweaving our reflections of ourselves on Earth, of scattering eyes upon it, and of scattering the Earth upon our eyes. It comes alive between yes and no, between what is and what is not, between science and non-science. And as soon as it becomes acquisitive, something egotistic...
it vanishes."
– Ian McCallum

If one pauses to consider one's place in life, it is clear that, as individuals and as a species, humans belong on this planet. Earth comes out of star dust, oceans come out of earth, Africa comes out of the oceans, and we come out of Africa. We are well versed to be full members of the universe. We also know through the science of physics and ecology that we are inextricably interconnected to all of life and that our existence depends on others' and earth's processes. However, we live in a constant state of forgetfulness, and cultural practices seek to wipe clean any memory of interdependence and replace it with separation, where we do not feel welcome and hence do not welcome others into a life of flourishing. For this reason, we need to hone our awareness of reality through the practice of Ecological Intelligence (EI). Birding is one such EI practice.

Ecological intelligence is the capacity to recognize the often-hidden web of connections between human activity and nature's systems, and the subtle complexities of their intersections, so that we may minimize harm and maximize flourishing for all. It is both an intellectual and an emotional expertise that strives for nourishing others as yourself, for caring for one is caring for all. There are multiple ways in which our lives are held together by the web of life. The elemental atoms within us came forth from the big bang, forming the first stars. Much later, when the dust of stars coalesced into Earth, the carbon, hydrogen, nitrogen, and oxygen parts of that dust arranged themselves into molecules. These molecules, such as water, first produced primordial seas, and then were processed through towering conifers, dinosaur blood, and Jesus' tears to come to rest in you. You who breathe today take in the oxygen that was once part of the bodies of fish, birds, and *Homo neanderthalis,* and they become you. We who live today exist because of those who lived before us, and because of those who live now alongside us.

We exist in a complex, dynamic, and coherent network. It may feel, at times, like a sticky mess where our allegiances are torn between ourselves and others. The reality, though, is more harmony than cacophony. In some ways our lives cannot help but sing in that harmony – we can't help but play out the nature that eons of evolution gave us. In other ways, though, we can train ourselves to better hear the harmonic subtleties and add our voice in a way that consciously supports the entire vast choir of existence.

Birding is part of this training. By paying attention to birds we discover the often-hidden interconnections of interdependent malfeasance. Once we train ourselves, we realize that birds near and far are in trouble. Species are declining at alarming rates and climate change produces extra stressors and challenges to which we are unsure the birds can adapt. One goal of birding though is not to experience shame, but to gain awareness about the mesh of interdependent malfeasance in which we all are stuck. Interdependent malfeasance is when one action or set of behaviors may also lead to a chain of harm that echoes through many lives and individuals. It may be hard for humans to see examples of harmful ecological behavior outside of our own actions, however, given our propensity to romanticize the concept of ecological balance and denigrate our own species. We tend to think that whatever another species does to harm another contributes to maintaining a habitat, but what *we* might do knocks things out of whack. In reality there is no such thing as ecological balance. Yes, there are fairly tightly woven pockets of interaction and interdependence, but these are always being rewoven as species evolve and the planet changes. In general, scientists know that ecosystems are more of a spiral or a wave, not ever in total balance, but always changing. Life came and went long before humans came into being; an estimated 99.9% of all species that ever existed are now extinct

During the Late Devonian (360 million years ago), the world's waters were teeming with extensive reef systems and marine biodiversity. But sea levels rose, giving some new species access to new environments. Some of these species were so numerous and dominant that they outcompeted other species, which resulted in a mass extinction in the seas and a collapse of reef systems and their entire disappearance from the world's oceans for 100 million years. It seems that humans are not the only ones to threaten reefs, yet we have the capability to not do so. We need to feel good that we do good, and can choose good, because it can have a large ripple impact. This counterbalances how bad we feel for the many ways we are involved in malfeasance. We need this countering effect, so we can have the reserves to reduce our harm, which also feels good.

So how can birds tell us of our interconnecting relations of harm with others? If you have a cat in your life and let them outdoors, they are most likely hunting, and this leads to death and suffering of wild birds and animals, as well as the diminishment of species whose populations are under threat. Having the cat outdoors also places him at risk for accidents, fights, and infectious disease, for himself and for others. If you elect to neuter your cat to reduce the risk of fighting, roaming, and more cats, the adopted cat is impacted by experiencing pain and not being able to live out the full potential of evolution's call to reproduce. Vaccinations are also momentarily painful, and in some cases can cause more long term hurt. If you keep your cat indoors, your needs for flourishing of life, as well as the cat's, might be impacted, as cats evolved for the outdoors. Feeding your cat also causes harm. Most likely your cat eats cat food that contains animal protein. A large percentage of store-bought cat food contains fish meal, which means that fish died and suffered, and also the ocean's populations of fish were put at risk. Other animal protein comes from animals raised in industrial farms where animals, such as cows and pigs, experience pain and suffering.

Even a simple bird feeder has implications, for we are not only benefiting birds when we feed them. The food placed in the feeders is grown, often intensively, replacing native habitat and employing the use of pesticides and herbicides. The food might also come from quite a distance, adding to climate change through the use of petroleum products in transportation, as well as during planting and harvesting. Bird feeders are often the source of infectious disease, even when cleaned thoroughly, as birds can transmit disease from one to other. Furthermore, predatory birds know about bird feeders, and visit them often to hunt and secure their own food. Inadequate placement of bird feeders can increase the risk of death due not only to predation, but also to window strikes as birds come and go to the feeders.

Knowing how easy it is to cause harm, we may adopt the precautionary principle that our actions cause harm and that we seek to never rend any single fragile thread in the web of

Guide #5: Birding to Nurture Life

life except through extreme necessity. We look not to harm, but to maximize the good that one single action of ours can produce. To do this, we become detectives to discover how we are connected to beneficence and malfeasance by knowing our ecology and being prepared to accept the reality of our interactions. In a sense we put on our scientist hats and our impartial observer robes as we minimize preconceived notions of wrong doing and right doing. The goal is not to look for blame, but to see how interrelated we are to the world with each breath, thought, and action. By looking for relationships, we enforce the reality of how we belong on this planet, for better or for worse, for ourselves and others. In the long run, I believe holding this awareness will not only be good for others, but for ourselves, for we are connected through nurturing and benefit.

When one individual or species is nurtured, these actions positively impact a plethora of species and ecological niches, and this is known as interdependent beneficeance. One example of this are top carnivores that are involved in trophic cascades. Trophic cascades are the changes that occur in an ecosystem by adding, removing or changing the behavior of top predators in a food web, which then impacts other predators, herbivores, and plants. For instance, when sea otters hunt sea urchins, this helps keep kelp forests healthy, which impacts a wide variety of species, including humans. Kelp forests help soften the impact of waves and currents in coastal areas. Humans, too, can offer benefit to many other species in one fell swoop. For example, we may have hunted with early wolves, who in turn benefited, so that they could then contribute to ecosystems through their impact on prey species, who further impact plant systems.

By being honest with ourselves and learning about others, we live authentically and flow with the reality of the world, instead of being imprisoned in how our culture in the past has thought of other species. We learn things that connect us to others through our common roots of star dust and DNA, and through basic shared and common needs. We all want to live, and live well, and in life seeking its full expression through each, we can experience profound belonging and awe. We are invited into a living world that is full of wonder and life-giving relationships possible at every moment. When we watch birds we nurture ourselves, and so grow our capacity to nurture others. Even as one walks through an urban setting, we can take in the throngs of other beings and see that the there is more to life than the superficial glance that writes off life as being made up of drab species living in a desert of biodiversity, as writes Mary Oliver in this excerpt of her poem, "Starlings in Winter."

Chunky and noisy,
but with stars in their black feathers,

they spring from the telephone wire
and instantly
they are acrobats
in the freezing wind...

...I am thinking now
of grief, and of getting past it;
I feel my boots
trying to leave the ground...

...I want to be improbable beautiful and afraid of nothing,
as though I had wings

Birding helps us embrace reality, not just of the world of birds, but of all existence. In the movie, "The Thin Red Line," the hero, a soldier in the South Pacific during World War II, muses as he discovers a dying parrot chick on the ground that had been blown out of her nest due to the bombs that were ensuring the mutual destruction of plant and animal life:

"One man looks at a dying bird and thinks there's nothing but answerable pain. Another man sees that same bird and feels the glory – feels something smiling through it."

We embrace reality, not to torture ourselves, but to nurture ourselves and others. Rev. Meredith Garmon, a Unitarian Universalist minister, explains how this way:

"Reality is never depressing. Being in denial, being out of touch with reality, pushing it out of consciousness, so that it has to sneak around, come at you from behind and crawl up your back (for reality eventually finds a way to get through to us), that's the source of depression. Struggling to resist irresistible reality - that's what triggers depression and stress. Reality is never depressing.

As a species we did not adopt the Ecospiritual Imperative to connect spiritually to nature in a way that would have empowered us, in joy, to preserve the Earth we knew. As a result, now we face the Ecospiritual Challenge to fashion what life we can on the new Earth. The Ecospiritual Challenge is to walk a third way: not denying the reality we face, and not retreating into everyone-for-herself-survivalism. It is the path of open-eyed and open-eared awareness, and also the path of connection to both nature and neighbor - not afraid to face reality, not avoiding needed knowledge because it's "depressing" and you'd rather not think about it. And at the same time not bunkering protectively. The Ecospiritual Challenge is to choose neither despair nor defense, but new community."

This "new community" is one where all belong and are connected and interdependent to each other, and to the whole. Birding brings us into a community and welcomes us to the family of life, again as exemplified in a poem by Mary Oliver, "Wild Geese."

You do not have to be good.
You do not have to walk on your knees for a hundred miles through the desert repenting.
You only have to love what the soft animal of your body loves.
Tell me about despair, yours, and I will tell you mine...

...Whoever you are, no matter how lonely, the world offers itself to your imagination, calls to you like the wild geese, harsh and exciting, over and over announcing your place in the family of things.

Liberating Wings

When despair for the world grows in me...I go and lie down where the wood drake rests in this beauty on the water, and the great heron feeds.
I come into the peace of wild things...
...For a time I rest in the grace of the world and am free.
– Wendell Berry

We bird so that all beings may be free. Tomás Manzanares, an indigenous Miskito leader in Honduras, explained it to me one day down at the river near his village. I was visiting his area to witness and stand in solidarity with the villages that wish to resist the overwhelming forces that seek to extract their trees, steal their wild parrots for the illegal wildlife trade, take their land, and impose violence, corruption, and the drug trade as a way of life. Tomás stood up to these forces that were destroying his ancestral lands. For his efforts, he made enemies who ambushed him one day, and he was shot four times. He nearly died. His whole village had to flee because they were likewise threatened with the loss of their lives. Yet, four months later he returned to the ghost-like village to work with me and others on parrot conservation. We had to hire a squad of soldiers from the Honduran military to accompany us and keep us safe. I asked him why he was willing to risk his life. He replied, "Doctora, everything is at risk so I am willing to risk everything. If the parrots don't make it, neither do my people."

I agree that we must take care of the most oppressed, and ourselves as well. To do so we need to get at the root causes that lead to domination, colonization, and injustice that cage us all. No matter where or how we live in the world, we each are subject to societal forces that imprison and wipe out humans and birds.

The beauty of birds reminds us of the beauty of this earth, and of ourselves. If we can remember that, we liberate ourselves as we liberate all life.

We strive to do so, for none are free until all are free.

Reflection Questions

Don't treat these questions like "homework" or a list that needs to be covered in its entirety. Instead, simply pick the one question that "hooks" you most and let it lead you where you need to go. These questions may help you understand birds as poetry, myth, symbol, and metaphor, and may also help you understand the birds around you and what they might mean for your life. So, which question is calling to you? Which one contains "your work"? You can use these questions for journaling, or to spark conversation with others. For all the readings that are not explicitly multispecies, ask yourself:

    a. How is the author addressing or not addressing a multispecies perspective?

    b. How would you add to these readings to have them address a multispecies perspective?

    c. Do the readings have more meaning to you with or without a multispecies perspective?

1. What do birds mean to you as symbol, myth, or metaphor?

2. What are your feelings towards actual birds? Fear? Appreciation? Awe? Worry?

3. Have you ever had an experience with birds or in nature that was transcendent or wondrous?

4. What helps you connect to nature, human animals, or other animals?

5. Do you experience any guilt or shame regarding the state of the world (such as with biodiversity loss, extinction, climate change)?

6. Do you experience any dissonance between how much you enjoy birds or other animals, and your individual behavior that might harm them (consumption of goods and food, transportation, housing, clothes, entertainment)?

7. How might you gain more freedom for yourself and others?

Weekly Nurture Nature Practices

A. Nurturing Ourselves: Walking meditation on a four-count cycle.

Walking meditation is a mindfulness practice. While outside watching birds, dedicate a part of your time to a walking meditation. Choose a level path or paved area without obstacles or tripping points. Walk in silence and as thoughts arise – judgments, plans, "to do lists" – observe all of these and let them go. Return to simply being, observing the path in front of you, the plants and birds around you. Many people time their breaths with their steps to help them still their inner chatter. They breath in over two to four steps, and breath out over the next two to four steps. To connect ever more greatly to birds, choose a four-count cycle for that is how birds breathe. With their internal air sacs, they can "store" fresh oxygenated blood, insuring that during every breath in and out fresh air surges through their lungs. It takes two breaths in and two breaths out if you are bird to exhale the original air taken in, making it a four-count cycle of respiration.

B. Deepening and Sharing Ourselves: Wonder of Birds

Every day for a week, look up some interesting facts about a bird species, or birds in general. Let yourself be curious as to the behavior and ecology of birds, and as you learn something new, say out loud, "wow!" with enthusiasm. Verbalizing this will help you experience wonder and awe, which is good for you. Then go share what you learned or experienced with others, eliciting if you can awe and wonder in them.

For instance, did you know that the bassian thrush of Australia hunts by directing a stream of flatulence toward the site of a worm find? The gas disturbs the worm and provokes movement. The thrush can then locate the worm and ingest it for a meal. Wow!

C. Moving from Inner to Outer Work

Birds nurture us so that we may nurture others. Make a list of what feeds you, especially in terms of being with birds and nature. Perhaps beauty is one way you are nurtured, perhaps hope another, as in this poem "Hope is the Thing with Feathers" by Emily Dickinson:

"Hope" is the thing with feathers -
That perches in the soul -
And sings the tune without the words -
And never stops - at all -

And sweetest - in the Gale - is heard -
And sore must be the storm -
That could abash the little Bird
That kept so many warm -

I've heard it in the chillest land -
And on the strangest Sea -
Yet - never - in Extremity,
It asked a crumb - of me.

Actually, birds do ask something of us. Make a list of how being in relationship with birds calls you to service to others. Pick one service action to do and do it this week.

Though their words are simple and few.
Listen, listen, they're calling to you.
Feed the birds, that's what they cry
While overhead the birds fill the skies.
– "Feed the Birds" from Mary Poppins

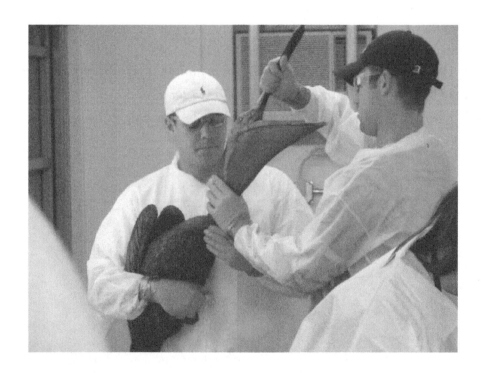

Other Suggested Practices

1. Join eBird (www.eBird.org) and start entering birds that you see during your normal routine, or when you purposely going out looking for birds. The data from the citizen scientists on eBird is helping us to cherish and conserve these species.

2. Pick one charity or nonprofit organization that helps birds and either donate or volunteer time there, such as at a local nature center or Audubon, which has both local and national chapters.

Resources

Books
- Jennifer Ackerman. *The Genius of Birds*. 2016.
- James H. Austin. *Living Zen Remindfully: Retraining Subconscious Awareness.* 2016.
- Jonathan Rosen. *The Life of the Skies: Birding at the End of Nature*. 2008.
- David Allen Sibley. *The Sibley Guide to Birds, 2nd Edition*. 2014.
- Noah Strycker. *The Thing with Feathers*. 2014.

Guide #6: Nature Poetry for Life

Nurture
Nature
Yours, Ours, Theirs, Earth's

Guide #6 Table of Contents

FORMAT FOR NURTURE NATURE COMMUNITY 112

READINGS:
Main Reading: Birding and Poetry in the USA 113
Additional Readings 118

REFLECTIONS
Reflection Questions 124

NURTURE NATURE PRACTICES
Weekly Nurture Nature Practices 125

RESOURCES 127

Published by One Earth Conservation, www.oneearthconservation.org
info@oneearthconservation.org

Please help us to continue to provide free resources for the public, such as this guide, by giving a tax-deductible donation to One Earth Conservation at: https://www.oneearthconservation.org/donate
All proceeds go to directly to helping the people and the parrots of the world.

Thanks to Rev. Meredith Garmon and Community Unitarian Universalist Congregation (http://www.cucwp.org/) for compiling some of these materials as part of their Journey Group program.

Photo credits: Photo on page 122 by Yongxinge

Format for Nurture Nature Community

We speak and listen deeply with our hearts and minds, allowing each to speak without interruptions, questions, or advice (unless solicited). The facilitator will help guide us in this so we can make the deepest connections possible to ourselves, other, earth, and earth's beings.

Before You Meet

Ask people to bring their favorite nature/animal poem or books, and samples of other poems in books or documents. Also ask people to read this booklet before they arrive and reflect upon what they learned and which reflection question seems the most relevant to them. Each should bring a copy of this booklet.

Arriving/Warm Up

As you arrive, make a name tag and draw a picture or write a word that symbolizes what animal or part of nature is meaningful or important to you. Share with one another why you wrote this word.

Opening Words

Look up and bring with you a copy of Mary Oliver's poem "Wild Geese"

Check In

What's been happening in your life? How is it with your nature (soul, spirit, body, relationships, multispecies community) today? (Pause between each sharing for 10 seconds, and have a minute of silence after all sharing.)

Shared Exploration

Review the readings and have each person briefly suggest an important learning from them that might benefit others (we teach one another).

Our Shared Nurture Nature Practice (Discussion and Reflection)

Have everyone read a favorite poem of theirs. If they didn't bring one, have them pick one from the poetry books that people have brought or in the additional readings. Invite each person to share what the poem means to them. Also, share and discuss any of the Reflection Questions.

Guide #6: Nature Poetry for Life

Our Nurture Nature Practice (Embodiment)

Nurturing Inner and Outer Wildness with a Walk

1.   Do a traditional walk (refer to Wild Walk Guide).

2.   Do #3 under "Nurture Nature Practices – Nurturing Our Community."

Next Steps

What does your deepening on this theme ask of you to do? Of us together?

Confirm facilitator, location, date/time and subject of next meeting.

Check Out

From everything we've shared during this time together, what overall message stands out for you?

What gratitude and affirmation would you like someone else to know?

Closing Words

"Kindness and awareness work together. Through awareness we understand the underlying beauty of everything and every being."

– Amit Ray

MAIN READINGS

Life of the Skies – Birds and Poetry in the USA
by Rev. Dr. LoraKim Joyner

Is there a bird inside of you, yearning for freedom, for meaning? Can poetry and birds help liberate you, and others? D.H. Lawrence wrote, "Birds are the life of the skies, and when they fly – they reveal the thoughts of the skies."

Their songs, too, can tell us nature's thoughts. Anthony de Mello wrote of what bird song can do for us:

"A Buddhist master is walking with the disciple and he accuses the master of hiding the secret of Zen from him.

Just then a bird called from the riverside.

The master asked, do you hear the bird?

Yes, said the disciple.

Well then you know I have hidden nothing from you.

Yes, said the disciple.

And then he was enlightened."

In watching birds, not just a lightening of the spirit is possible, but something fiercer and not all that comfortable to behold. For when birds tell us of meaning, they tell us not just of life, but also of death. And it's in that crucible held by feathered wings that we can be held in both beauty and tragedy and make meaning of our lives.

Jonathan Rose, author of *The Life of the Skies – Birding at the End of Nature,* says the reason why there are some 50 million bird watchers in this country is because birds are the last remaining wild animals that are abundantly visible to us. They are the windows into all of wild nature, and our own wild nature as well.

So, we lost dinosaurs along the way for the dynamite soaring birds of today, and now we are losing them too, at our own hands, and it's not clear what new life might arise. It's hard as a bird watcher to not be aware of their dwindling numbers and not to despair. Once there were hundreds of thousands of Carolina parakeets, and 2 billion passenger pigeons in the U.S and now they are gone. The parakeet and pigeon went extinct for many reasons, and tragically the last birds succumbed to collectors. The only nest of Carolina parakeet eggs, long dead, is housed at the Florida Museum of Natural History. They were turned in by a poacher who would not reveal the location of this last nest until long after the parents died, and subsequently the entire species. I was given a private tour so that I could see them, and when the curator opened the drawers of the storage cabinet, it was as if I had walked into a holy temple, and like any place of homage, life and death were inseparable.

In our primate minds, the urge to kill and the urge to conserve are so closely linked, death never far from life, as experienced so acutely with a flying bird of life easily dead due to the fragility of their hollow bones, air sacs, and paper-thin feathers. John James Audubon saw a monkey kill his parrot. He mused that it is this image that caused him to study and paint birds with pleasure, and to do so he killed thousands of birds. The arts, painting, prose, and poetry all can tell us of life, death, and the wildness within.

The wild primate lives inside of us all. We hunt as we look for birds through our binoculars, and we are haunted by a lifestyle that is disappearing earth's birds. In the early twentieth century, President Teddy Roosevelt heard reports about plume hunters wiping out bird populations in Florida and created Pelican Island, which was the first time the federal government set aside land for the sake of wildlife. Roosevelt was a great conservationist, not "in spite of the fact that he was a hunter, but because he was one. He never discounted the human urge to destroy, since he indulged in that urge so zealously himself. Rather accepting it as a given of human nature, he allowed that knowledge to inform his understanding of the necessity of check and balances of human rapacity." (from *The Life of the Skies: Birding at the End of Nature*, by Jonathan Rosen)

Knowing who we are and what we might do, based on our understanding of our place in communities of mixed species, are key religious questions. Birds help us know of our sacred reality, our divine possibility, and how we must arise out of the ashes of our burning human greed. And poetry of birds brings this message of their quieting song to us.

Harold Bloom, who studied American religious poetry, found in Emerson, Thoreau, Whitman, Adams, Frost, and Dickinson the image that the risen Jesus is in each of us – that each of us as individuals can bring salvation to this world through the blessing of our very being. John James Audubon's paintings captured this in his anthropomorphized birds. They don't look like birds as much as they look like humans with feathers. He melds birds with humans – wild nature, beauty without end, amen.

Walt Whitman perhaps best portrayed nature and birds as lived religion. As a boy, Whitman listened to a pair of mockingbirds one summer. Then one of the pair died and the remaining bird sang throughout the night. The young Whitman went out into the night to listen to this song and was changed forever. Later he said, "Now in a moment I know what I am for." He wrote about this episode in his famous poem, "Out of the Cradle Endlessly Rocking."

Jonathan Rosen writes, "In its fusion of the human and the animal, and in its depiction of an entire country through animal symbols, it is a kind of poetic extension of Audubon's paintings…" The expanse of North America birthed a nation of poets and a new religion that was based at once both on infinite beauty and its diminishment, and both on the frailty of bodies and the divine light and possibility in them.

Emerson, too, melds human experience with birds. Drawn to Sufism, Emerson writes of the *Conference of the Birds*, one of the most central of all Sufi texts. In this text, birds undertake a spiritual journey and show us the way of Emerson's Transcendentalism, a kind of homegrown American Sufism. We are the image of God, and divinity reflects from our souls ever more brightly as we work to polish our inner mirror.

Colleague to Emerson, Emily Dickinson compared birding to church, and preferred birding. It's a tough call. The point is birds and church-like activities are just some of the ways to grow more connected, more aware, and more whole, which is the eternal light ever shining in the darkness.

Robert Frost wrote in the 20th century, a time of darkness, death and extinction. Robert Pack in his book, *Belief and Uncertainty in the Poetry of Robert Frost,* writes that Frost's poem, "The Ovenbird," poses this: The question that he (the bird) frames in all but words is what to make of a diminished thing.

What are we to make of our diminishing lives through age, illness, death, the loss of biodiversity, and climate change? Hope isn't the thing with feathers – it's us. We are the ones who can learn to know ourselves and the world around us and take intentional steps forward into a future of abundant life.

In the U.S.A. there is an interesting connection between birds and Unitarian Universalists (UUs), who manifested an early version of nature religion in this country and sought to know who they are through birds and to respond accordingly because of their long history with birds and nature religion. You could say that UUs are part of a Republic of Feathers that has many UU members. Whitman, Dickinson, Thoreau, and Frost had strong Unitarian Universalist connections. UUs also clearly claim as their own Emerson, the two Adams Presidents and Thomas Jefferson who kept a pet mockingbird in the White House Study.

The people of the U.S.A. are the descendants of all this birding and nature activity, helping one another face the darkness around us and in us all, seeking to free ourselves from senseless suffering through joy. Birding and poetry are but a few ways to take up an intentional practice that asks us to look within at our inner demons and look outward in acknowledgement that though we may be or feel alone, we are interconnected to all of life.

Thoreau, the patron saint of backyard birders, exhibited the paradox of birding and our kind by loving isolation and craving connection. He wrote:

"Each new year is a surprise to us. We find that we had virtually forgotten the note of each bird, and when we hear it again, it is remembered like a dream, reminding us of a previous sate of existence. The voice of nature is always encouraging. In a bird, we meld the past with the dream of the future."

Birding is the synthesis of individuals and communities, of art and science, and of secularism and religion. Watching birds allows us to live in a symbolic world that is also scientific. We do not lose our rational mind, but instead find our wondrous mind in seeing wonder around us. Birding perhaps seems such a small thing to do, but small gestures can save the world, as can small groups upon wooded or sandy trail. For it is there on the path where beauty is all around us, as is death, that we can let loose our joy. Joy does not lead us to "escape the world, but to fly free in it, to embrace it with all its suffering and all its wonder and creative powers." (David Spangler).

To embrace all is no easy path. A number of years ago I went for a short walk to get my mail. There flew across me a Cooper's hawk carrying a red-bellied woodpecker screaming its final song. The hawk could barely fly, so burdened was it with the crying pitiful bird. I wanted to run after it and tear the beautiful dying thing from its talons, and yet was also mesmerized by the beauty of the successful hunt. I was not alone in reacting to this drama, for a red-tailed hawk was chasing the Cooper's hawk, either to steal the prey or the life of the smaller hawk. Following these two predators was a mixed-species flock of song birds, their calls fierce for their size. In me was a turning of the gut, a heart-wrenching glimpse of reality where all moments consist of inseparable life and death. In that one moment, I knew what I am for. I am here to do as Mary Oliver says, to love all things dearly as my life depends on it and then to let them go, let them go.

We all are burdened with dying things. For a good part of my life I have been a bird veterinarian and I know the stark truth that the desire to have bird beauty in our homes is killing off the wild birds and causing much suffering to those held captive. I've handled Spix Macaws, which are now extinct in the wild, due largely to collectors who desired these startlingly blue beings. In my career as a bird veterinarian, I worked for three of the four largest bird collections in the world. I did this, so I could be close to beauty and hence I captured my joy, binding the world to my desires with resulting loss and suffering. I am the monkey with parrot blood on her hands, the hawk with a dying bird in its talons, and the dove with a rising spirit of joy that cannot be caged.

In the movie, *The Thin Red Line* based on John James' novel the hero says, "One man looks at a dying bird and sees nothing but unanswerable pain, and another looks at the same bird and feels the glory, feels something smiling through it."

In our American lives, awash with death and loss, there is a rising hope, as captured by American's first bard, Walt Whitman. Invigorated by nature's expanse in America, he came to know who he was and what we all could be – a rising of the human spirit even in the midst of our folly and foibles.

116

ADDITIONAL READINGS

"The Poetry of the Earth is Never Dead"
from *Can Poetry Save the Earth? A Field Guide to Nature Poems* by John Felstiner

By "earth" I don't so much mean our planet, which will keep spinning till the sun gives out, but the natural world we're both part of and apart from. If poems touch our full humanness, can they quicken awareness and bolster respect for this ravaged resilient earth we live on?

"Care in Such a World"
from *Can Poetry Save the Earth? A Field Guide to Nature Poems* by John Felstiner

Can poems help, when the times demand environmental science and history, government leadership, corporate and consumer moderation, nonprofit activism, and local initiatives? Why call on the pleasures of poetry, when the time has come for an all-out response.

Homo sapiens, a recent arrival, has to refigure its place on earth, much as the Copernican revolution upset our geocentric universe. Are we a part or apart? The ways we speak of environmental and ecological concerns reflect these jostling mindsets. Should water and wildland be managed for or protected from people? Environmental and ecological thinking, in poems and at large, ranges the ground between what we call civilization and wilderness. Egocentric versus ecocentric: nature poetry lives by the tension.

Can poetry save the earth? For sure, person by person, our earthly challenge hangs on the sense and spirit that poems can awaken.

So much depends on seeing the things of our world afresh by saying them anew… Poetry more than any other kind of speech reveals the vital signs and warning signs of our tenancy on earth.

American Religious Poems
by Harold Bloom

The United States, already a plutocracy, flickers these days towards theocracy. A theocratic America doubtless will distinguish between sacred and secular utterances, but

Whitmanian democracy fuses them in the divinity of the self, which is our native understanding of the Resurrection as an escape from history, that is to say, from European time. The Resurrection is not a mediated event for American Religionists. Our prime shaman (Whitman) of the American Religion affirms the Blessing of more life. Death, for Walt Whitman, was an innocence of the earth, and no false sign or symbol or malice. These days we live not in the great poem of Whitmanian democracy, but in an America that fuses plutocracy and theocracy. The ruin or bland that we see in nature, Emerson prophesied, is in our own eye, and therefore we behold opacity, and not transparency. Returning to Walt Whitman, forever the ultimate American even as he is our Adam (he repudiates non-American religion by these statements): "Death is night, the mother and the sea; judgment is a horrible fiction, and there was never any more Heaven or Hell, then here and now." Whitman is the American difference, the herald to the future, if we do not destroy our future.

A Poetry Handbook: A Prose guide to Understanding and Writing Poetry
by Mary Oliver

If Romeo and Juliet had made appointments to meet, in the moonlight-swept orchard, in all the peril and sweetness of conspiracy, and then more often than not failed to meet – one or the other lagging, or afraid or busy elsewhere – there would have been no romance, no passion, none of the drama for which we remember and celebrate them. Writing a poem is not so different – as it is a kind of possible love affair between something like the heart (that courageous but also shy factory of emotion) and the learned skills of the conscious mind. They make appointments with each other, and keep them, and something begins to happen. Or, they make appointments with each other but are casual and often fail to keep them: count on it, nothing happens.

"Poetry By Heart"
by Rev. Meredith Garmon

"Poetry is when an emotion has found its thought and the thought has found words." (Robert Frost)

"Poetry is not only dream and vision; it is the skeleton architecture of our lives. It lays the foundations for a future of change, a bridge across our fears of what has never been before." (Audre Lorde)

Read poetry. When a poem stands out for you as a favorite, stay with it. Copy it into a "favorite poems" notebook. Learn it by heart. Repeat it often, murmuring to yourself or reciting it to appropriate others.

Unitarian Universalist ministers Rev. Harry Scholefield and Rev. Laurel Hallman have articulated a spiritual practice Hallman calls "Living by Heart." Collect and write down poems, songs, stories that have spoken lyrically and wisely to human beings since time immemorial. Scholefield called these words and music the "Singing River" that represented for him the continual dawning of the human spirit.

By recording words of wisdom that have personal meaning and "living" with them until they become one's "heart wisdom," those words come to occupy a place beyond memory. When you live with a poem so intimately that it enters your heart, it becomes a constant resource, companion, and guide. Years and innumerable experiences accumulate, yet the rhymes and rhythms we stored deep in our brains stay with us.

The pace of contemporary life is often hectic and can seem unmanageable. Taking time to take in, to receive and hold wisdom in a form that can be accessed and used as a reminder of what holds our life can re-focus us in a helpful way.

"Poetry is a particularly rich genre because it speaks to both head and heart. It has carried the wisdom and stories of the ages. Think of the Illiad, the ancient Greek tale that has served for centuries as a metaphor for the journey away and back to self; consider the Psalms in Bible, poetry that carried the ancient Jews through the tribulations of exile and on to the promised land; recall the work of Shakespeare the greatest secular literature of all time that leaves no aspect of the human condition untouched. Consider the work of Mary Oliver and Wendell Berry and May Sarton and Denise Levertov and ee cummings other contemporary poets used liberally in our UU worship to celebrate the wonders of the natural world and our place in it." (Rev. Karen Gustafson)

Words of poetry and poetic, wise prose, taken to heart, become, as Hallman says "the words that sustain, inspire, and give voice to my life. They are words that call me back to a place of gratitude when the perspective that I face is dissatisfaction and disappointment."

Some dozen or so years ago I watched a video of Hallman and Scholefield describing the life of spiritual deepening and, particularly, this practice of learning poetry by heart. I began to hand copy favorite poems into a small spiral-bound notebook dedicated to that purpose. Below is a sampling of some of my "heart wisdom" words. Perhaps some of them will also resonate with you and get you started on a path of gathering words to live by. Gather the words, and the words will gather you.

Excerpt from "Wild Geese"
by Mary Oliver

You do not have to be good.
You do not have to walk on your knees
For a hundred miles through the desert, repenting.
You only have to let the soft animal of your body
love what it loves…
…the world offers itself to your imagination,
calls to you like the wild geese, harsh and exciting –
over and over announcing your place
in the family of things.

Excerpt from "The Guest House"
by Jelauddin Rumi

This being human is a guest house.
Every morning a new arrival…

…Be grateful for whatever comes.
because each has been sent
as a guide from beyond.

Excerpt from "The Peace of Wild Things"
by Wendell Berry

…I go and lie down where the wood drake
rests in his beauty on the water, and the great heron feeds.
I come into the peace of wild things…

Excerpt from "A Gift"
by Denise Levertov

...in the emptiness of your hands,
songbird eggs that can still hatch...
... Yes, perhaps
this gift is your answer.

"Prayer to the Rabbit God"
By Rev. Meredith Garmon

the rabbit god made bunnies
as morning brightened into day.
she gave them a green planet to eat,
made them love to hump
like rabbits
and love their babies.

bunnies make bunnies faster than plants grow, she noticed.
so, as evening darkened into night,
the rabbit god made foxes.

predation, she said,
will give my lovelies
sharp ears,
beautiful speed,
a touch of cleverness.
let them be grateful for the red fur death
and the fear that makes them so alert.

thus the rabbit god became the fox god too.
bodies are made of nutrients,
there being no other way to make them.
how could there not be carnivores?

dear god of hunter and of hunted,
i, too a body made of food, pray
to be eaten rather than outconsume providence
to love
the beauty of my fears.

Bejing Rabbit God

Reflection Questions

Don't treat these questions like "homework" or a list that needs to be covered in its entirety. Instead, simply pick the one question that "hooks" you most and let it lead you where you need to go. The goal of these questions is not to help analyze or come to a final answer. The questing itself brings forth "answers" and knowing deeply embedded in your being. So, which question is calling to you? Which one contains "your work"? You can use these questions for journaling, or to spark conversation with others. For all the readings that are not explicitly multispecies, ask yourself:

  a. How is the author addressing or not addressing a multispecies perspective?

  b. How would you add to these readings to have them address a multispecies perspective?

  c. Do the readings have more meaning to you with or without a multispecies perspective?

1. How do you feel about poetry as a whole? Do poems resonate with you? If so, do they call to you as you read them, share them, or write them?? Why or why not?

2. How do you define poetry?

3. Have you experienced or learned of how other species engage in poetry or metaphorical language or behavior?

4. How might nature or other beings be considered poetry?

5. Who is your favorite poet? Why?

6. What is your favorite poem? Why?

7. Are there particular styles or eras of poetry that you enjoy more?

8. Have any poems left you inspired? Touched? Whole? Why or how?

9. Have any poems left you down, sad, or irritated? Why or how?

10. Have you ever tried to write poetry? How was that for you?

11. What do nature poems tell you about what it means to be a human animal in a multispecies community and what might be the human compassionate response to that understanding?

12. What do poems tell you about birth, growth, change, pain, loss, and death? What do poems tell you about the reality of existence? What do poems tell you about the mysterious unknown of existence? Can you think of concrete examples?

13. How does poetry interact with the metaphoric symbolic nature of your being with the scientific rational part?

14. Do you feel that poetry could be a spiritual practice, for you, or for others?

15. Does poetry inspire you to action or some intersectional justice endeavor? (Intersectional justice is working to understand and ease injustice in one particular case, while also recognizing how one particular injustice intersects with others through the related systems of oppression, domination, or discrimination.)

Weekly Nurture Nature Practices

A. Nurturing Yourself

A. Pick a collection of poems, perhaps from this booklet, or from the internet or a book. Choose poetry that speaks of nature and beings. Choose a beautiful, restful place to read a poem. Breathe three times deeply and then read a poem silently to yourself. Shut your eyes and breathe three times deeply. What do you see and feel in your inner being? Breathe three times deeply. Now read the poem again, this time aloud. Keeping your eyes open as you breathe deeply, what do you see and feel? Now let your thoughts wander for a couple of minutes. Breathe three times again, and then take up pen and paper and journal. Write whatever comes to you. Also, you may choose to respond to the reflection questions, below or write your own reflection questions.

1. What is the poem asking of you?
2. What does the poem invite you to see and feel?
3. Who are the characters in the poem and what are they doing? Why?

4. Where is there beauty or benefit in the poem? In your life?

5. Where is there tragedy or harm in the poem? In your life?

6. What is the poem asking of you?

7. What actions or behaviors does the poem invite?

8. What other reflections do these poems elicit?

Repeat this every day for a week. At the end of the week, pick one poem that was the most meaningful for you and memorize it.

B. Over a period of time, collect a poem for each kind of being or habitat. Paste them into a book or computer-generated document. Consider illustrating them or using clip art or photos. As you add poems, ask yourself why you chose this poem and what it means to you. This could be an activity to do with other people of all ages – a community project.

B. Nurture Others

1. Invite one or more other people to join you and have a short poetry time together. Invite them to share their favorite nature poem, and you share yours. Go through the reflection questions in this booklet and discuss what the poems mean for you.

2. With nature poems in mind that you have read or journaled about, pick one specific beneficial action that the poem invites you to consider, and go do it. For instance, you may have ready Mary Oliver's "Wild Geese," and will feel inspired to invite another person to go birding with you where there are geese. You might also read up on the conservation status of geese or their needs and make a donation or volunteer for an organization that helps geese or ducks.

C. Nurturing Our Communities is Nurturing Yourself

1. Consider sharing your favorite nature poems in a community setting. Perhaps you can introduce a meeting with a poem, or part of a poem, or share it as a "blessing" before a meal.

2. Donate a book of nature poetry to a social justice or community assistance organization or shelter (such as temporary housing, a dog shelter, a nature center).

3. Invite others on a "Wild Walk" and then after the walk, write a poem together about

what you experienced. Someone begins with a line, which everyone writes down. Then provide time and quiet for each to write a line that will go next. Choose the line that goes next and then have everyone suggest a third line. Continue until the group feels that the poem has captured the nature within and without.

Resources

Books

- Harold Bloom and Jesse Zuba (editors). *American Religious Poems.*
- John Felstiner. *Can Poetry Save the Earth: A Field Guide to Nature Poems.*
- LoraKim Joyner. "A Year's Rising" (blog of Mary Oliver Poems). http://yearsrisingmaryoliver.blogspot.com/.
- Mary Oliver. *A Poetry Handbook. A Prose Guide to Understanding and Writing Poetry.*
- Mary Oliver (many, many other poetry books).
- Robert McDowell. *Poetry as Spiritual Practice: Reading, Writing, and Using Poetry in Your Daily Rituals, Aspirations, and Intentions.*
- Jonathan Rosen. *The Life of the Skies: Birding at the End of Nature.*

Guide #7: Spiritual Animals

Guide #7 Table of Contents

FORMAT FOR NURTURE NATURE COMMUNITY...................................130

READINGS:
Main Readings: What is Spiritual Intelligence?............................131
               Developing a Heart of Lightness......................132
Additional Readings...137

REFLECTIONS
Reflection Questions..145

NURTURE NATURE PRACTICES
Weekly Nurture Nature Practices...............................146

RESOURCES...147

Published by One Earth Conservation, www.oneearthconservation.org
info@oneearthconservation.org

Please help us to continue to provide free resources for the public, such as this guide, by giving a tax-deductible donation to One Earth Conservation at: https://www.oneearthconservation.org/donate
All proceeds go to directly to helping the people and the parrots of the world.

Thanks to Rev. Meredith Garmon and Community Unitarian Universalist Congregation (http://www.cucwp.org/) for compiling some of these materials as part of their Journey Group program.

Format for Nurture Nature Community

We speak and listen deeply with our hearts and minds, allowing each to speak without interruptions, questions, or advice (unless solicited). The facilitator will help guide us in this, so we can make the deepest connections possible to ourselves, others, earth, and earth's beings.

Arriving/Warm Up

As you arrive, make a name tag and draw a picture or write a word representing where you have experienced a deep connection or had a spiritual experience with another species.

Opening Words

"Accepting our kinship with all life on earth is not only solid science...in my view, it's also a soaring spiritual experience."

– Neil deGrasse Tyson

Check In

Share your name, why you are here today and where you are from. If inclined, share where have you recently experienced a sense of transcending yourself with another species. If your group meets for a longer time, and the group is not large, share what's been happening in your life. How is it with your soul, spirit, mind, body today?

Shared Exploration

Review the main readings and have each person briefly suggest an important learning from them that might benefit others (we teach one another)

Watch the video, "How to be Ultraspiritual" (link in Resources section)

Our Shared Nurture Nature Practice (Discussion and Reflection)

You are invited to share a story from your own life – a relationship you have with another species (flora or fauna) that helped you forget yourself and connect to the larger world. Discuss what these stories and resources in this guide mean to you (to guide reflection – see Reflection Questions)

Our Nurture Nature Practice (embodiment)

Nurturing Our Spirituality with a Walk (#3 Weekly Nurture Nature Practices under Nurturing Yourself)

Next Steps

What does your deepening on this theme ask of you to do? Of us together?

Confirm facilitator, location, date/time and subject of next meeting

Check Out

From everything we've shared during this time together, what overall message stands out for you?

What gratitude and affirmation would you like someone else to know?

Closing Words

"We are spiritual animals, forever connected beyond our conscious knowing to infinite beauty to all life around us."

– LoraKim Joyner

MAIN READINGS

What is Spiritual Intelligence
Rev. Dr. LoraKim Joyner

Whoever you are, no matter how lonely,
the world offers itself to your imagination,
calls to you like the wild geese, harsh and exciting –
over and over announcing your place
in the family of things.
– Mary Oliver

Spiritual Intelligence is the ability to transcend individual ego concerns and perspectives by connecting to that which is greater than the self, fostering wisdom, acceptance, compassion, presence, and mindfulness. The previous four intelligences have also been about connecting to something bigger than ourselves and nurturing a greater sense of compassion, so they too contribute to spiritual intelligence.

The goal with this intelligence is to intentionally loosen the sense of self and increase our conscious and subconscious knowing that you are other bodies, all bodies, small and large, each and all. Empathy with yourself, with another human, with other species, and with the ecological web of relationships have each built upon one another, so that you can enter the realm of being not just one with the all, but all. You/I/she/he/it/we/they are not separate from others or the all of life, but simply one organ, one cell, or one grain of sand in existence that makes up reality.

There are many ways to grow in spiritual intelligence, both intentionally and accidentally, all of which can be summed up as: Taking the Big View. It's as if you are the big watcher, embracing the earth and all her beings with your empathy, connection, and understanding. There is no good or bad, right or wrong, better or worse, there just is. There is no story of what happened to me, or what I did, or what they did or thought; everything just is.

Now clearly, we cannot function as discrete beings in our daily lives, making decisions made wholly out of this frame of reference. There is an "I" and an "us" that we strive to concretely care for and take specific steps to ensure flourishing. We make judgments, either consciously or subconsciously, to move towards satisfaction and away from harm in our life. This is necessary and good for us, and for all.

What spiritual practices ask us to consider is what our days might look like if we also carried with us another remarkable perspective: *I am the beautiful whole watching all the beautiful beings. Each and all are so very precious. Even though harm and tragedy abound, beauty and worth never diminish, both connecting everything into a living whole.*

It might just be that our thoughts and actions slowly realign so that we grow in beauty and belonging. In knowing ever more strongly that we belong and are welcome on earth, we can welcome all others into the family of life, and nurture them accordingly.

Developing a Heart of Lightness
Rev. Dr. LoraKim Joyner

Spirituality is a journey into the human heart. You've all been on this journey before and know the depths of human nature. I wonder if your journey has been like Marlow's, a character in Joseph Conrad's *Heart of Darkness*? Marlow traveled deeper and deeper into the Congo looking for another character, the petty tyrant Kurtz, and saw the tragedy of humanity all around him. Do you travel similarly, looking not for Kurtz, but for hurts? Do you see, like Marlow, the darkness of our souls as we subjugate others, fall prey to illness and death, and strip and injure the land to gain wealth? But even Marlow, as he went deeper into darkness, saw beauty all around him in the jungle. The messiness and complexity of human nature is a jungle, and it's beautiful. So perhaps on your journey to the heart, you see instead lightness. You imagine your beauty connected to the beauty around, a woven fabric of life that lifts you up no matter your burdens.

What is in your heart today? Darkness, which might be fear? Perhaps you feel lightness, which might be love, because many little wonderful things are now going right. Writes Joseph Conrad:

> "These little things make all the great difference. When they are gone you must fall back upon your own innate strength, upon your own capacity for faithfulness. Of course, you may be too much of a fool to go wrong – too dull even to know you are being assaulted by the powers of darkness. Or you may be such a thunderingly exalted creature as to be altogether deaf and blind to anything but heavenly sights and sounds. Then the earth for you is only a standing place – and whether to be like this is your loss or your gain I won't pretend to say. But most of us are neither one nor the other."

We know of darkness and we know of light. We know fear and we know love. We have choice, which one we allow to fill our heart. The poet Jean Latimer writes:

> *There is a moment in time when the soul chooses love over fear. It may take eons to reach that point, but when it comes, it sweeps away all distrust, all suffering and judgment. We can prepare for it by practicing some simple techniques:*

The first technique is, as Latimer continues: *We practice feeling everything, so that when love comes, we feel it fully.* That is not easy. One spiritual teacher once told me, life isn't about feeling comfortable, it's about feeling everything. We feel everything, not to live in a maelstrom of overwhelming emotions, but in fact, to ease through our emotions so we can choose love over fear. What we want to do is to be in tune with our bodies and emotions, so we know what it is we need to best serve life in the current situation. But it's hard to know what we need.

I gave a workshop once on connecting feelings to needs, and to do so without trying to judge the other person as wrong for feeling, needing, or doing what they were doing. A mother came back to me after lunch break, and said, "It worked!" She had a car full of kids and her young daughter was screaming and crying and getting ready for a full-scale tantrum or fight with the other children. The mom said, "Instead of getting irritated with her for acting out, I tried to guess what she needed. She's so young, she might not know. So, I asked, "Are you hungry?" She said, "Yes," already calmer. "Okay, we'll be at the restaurant soon." The child rode the rest of the way peacefully.

We're all hungry for life to flourish abundantly in our lives, work, and relationships, and sometimes it helps to have someone help us figure out what we need. What we need can be so very simple. If you're like the average American, you are short on sleep. So, the next time you're about ready to blow up at someone or something, consider taking a nap, or eating or drinking something.

Here's another insight to blow ups. It's the 90/10 rule. If you are having a sustained emotional reaction to a situation, only 10% is from the actual real-time situation and 90% of its coming from experiences in your past. Once the stimulus is gone, feelings only last about 90 seconds, unless you continue to relive the situation. You keep thinking about the situation, because an emotional process center of your brain, the amygdala, keeps firing. It keeps firing because it's not so good at telling time. It just remembers "fear" from past situations, gets all wound up, and then hogs all the blood sugar in the brain so your higher function can't make a choice about how to address what you need in the moment.

You can calm the amygdala by having awareness of the current situation. Ask yourself, "what do I need now?" not "what did I need all those previous times in my life?" This gives us a chance to actually work with people on something they can help you with now, current needs, instead of them trying to guess what it is they can do to calm the wounded child before them. We all carry the wounds of the past – sexism, racism, genocide – it's in us all. I don't want to make light of that. But we can choose what we feel and think, so we don't blame others for our discomfort or think of them as evil doers. Instead we see them as fellow strugglers on the path as we take responsibility for our own feelings.

Latimer's poem goes on to say: *We practice mindfulness, so that when love comes, it is sustained by the discipline of choice not to indulge the small mind's need to negate and judge.* Mindfulness allows us to choose. Thinking of what we feel and need is one way to bring awareness to the current moment. By doing this, we can choose how we feel, and how we feel and think of others.

Want to try it here? I have a little exercise that shows how we can choose what we feel. I invite you to imagine a recent time when you were irritated, upset, sad, or disappointed. Now write a sentence about that experience. For example, I might write, "When I read in the paper about a certain political party I was so upset, because they always seem to lie." Don't hold back on what you are thinking – just let it rip! Now, when I say go, repeat that sentence (out loud or to yourself) that you wrote over and over again. When I say stop, do so. Ready? Go!......Now stop. Now think about what your body was doing during this time? Were you frowning? Were facial muscles tense? Your eyebrows knit? How about your shoulders? Were they tense or closed in? How about your stomach? Was it tight or aching? How was your breathing? Were you holding your breath or breathing shallowly?

Now imagine the same experience. This time, think of your needs that are not being met in the situation. Then fill in this sentence with the need: "I really love it when I experience _____." For example, I might write, "I really love it when I experience honesty." When I say go, repeat this sentence over and over again, as you did previously. Ready? Go!.....Now stop. What was your body doing this time? Any changes? Many of you probably felt a relaxation of the face, shoulders, and stomach. Maybe you were smiling, breathing more deeply, and felt peaceful.

This exercise demonstrates how we can change our feelings by translating an experience into needs. By thinking of needs we move towards connecting to life and are more open to life, without blaming ourselves or others. Our very body language tells us how we can open to others instead of closing off connection.

One final technique is: *we practice embracing that which we hate – our diseases, addiction, and troubles – so that love is felt wholly.*

Does this mean we must embrace cancer? Dementia? Death? That's going to take a lot of practice. Where can we do this? A supportive group setting is one place to do this, because we ask each other to love our neighbors as ourselves. Again, this is easier said than done, as portrayed in the following joke.

One Sunday morning a partner was shaking his spouse awake. "Honey, wake up, you'll be late for church." To which she responded, "But I don't wanna go. The people don't like me, they are mean to me, and the sermons are boring. Why do I have to go?" He replied, "Because you're the minister."

This kind of dynamic doesn't happen just in congregations in the United States, but in religions the world over. A Pew study in the 1980's found that people who consider themselves religious, that is, they regularly attend mosque, temple, or church, are generally less compassionate than the general public. This is not such good news. However, it's hopeful to note that, out of the people who consider themselves religious, 8% are far more compassionate than the general public. That's about one in 13. So, if you consider yourself religious, look at six people to your right, and six people to your left – you will be the only one who isn't a jerk.

That voice that considers others jerks – that's who we are. We evolved to discern and to judge. Love that. But have you a choice about which energy you chose to act out of, so that when *the moment of love comes we are swept away.*

Love can come in a moment, this very next moment, and it can change everything. A number of years ago my sister told me of a dream she had about a man with whom she worked. They did not get along and she often left meetings frustrated, hurt, and near tears. Then in the dream, the man appeared to her as the most beautiful person in the world. She felt unconditional love for him. So, when she awoke and went into work the next day, she greeted him gladly and did so over the next couple of weeks. He slowly began to change, and soon they started to get along quite well.

I once had a dream like that too. I dreamt about a person who was just a friend of mine. But in the dream, I loved him in the romantic sense. So, when I woke up, I was in love with him. We ended up marrying a few years later. That was husband number one, and it turns out that marrying him wasn't such a good choice after all. I bring this up to show that when we experience love, there are no demands on how we should act with another. We don't have to continue to work with them, marry them, or be nice to them. By loving them though, we see their beauty and this opens up possibilities of how we might have more satisfying relationships and experiences. By loving them, we have more choices on how to act.

We can choose to give love and compassion back to a bruised and aching world. If we show compassion, others do. It is catching. Scientists have designed experiments to see if and how compassion spreads from one person to another and to groups. They found that it does. Our positive emotions also impact other species. In one study, humans who raised baby parrots took an empathy test. Birds who were handled by humans with greater empathy were less stressed in their environment than those who were handled by humans with less empathy.

Changing how we feel will help others, but will this goal fix everything? It won't. My sister took care of my mother in her last year of life. It was a difficult relationship, considering my mother's anger and dementia. My sister longed to have the same kind of dream she had about her coworker with my mother, so the relationship could be as loving and open as possible. Sometimes we just can't make the shift.

135

What we can do is practice being loving and open when our needs are so not being met. Sometimes, we don't want our lives to be intertwined with people whose worth we struggle to see. But that doesn't mean that beauty isn't staring you right in the face everywhere you turn. Just look up at the stars and know you belong. You who are 2.5% Neanderthal, and 50% banana. You are beautiful. Don't you think it's time we started acting like it?

You can't do it every moment, but there is hope you can do it in the next moment. Remember the feeling and thought exercise we did? We can choose our thoughts and one moment can change everything. We can choose to bring lightness to our beings and our days. We can choose to create more moments like that, and if we do, we get a movement, and then a symphony.

Religious communities are shrinking all over the US. There was a video on YouTube that caught people's imagination, where a man said, "I love Jesus but hate religion." We so often hear, "I'm spiritual, but not religious." People the world over are tiring of religion, because of its suspected hypocrisy and its propensity to serve those who already have too much power and privilege. Well, we humans are hypocrites and we migrate to power and privilege. But if we commit to do the deep, painful work of loving ourselves as our neighbors, people may very well flock to our communities that intentionally help nurture one another and heal the world.

Here's the trick. This work can't be done alone. There is too much out there pushing against it. We back slide. We lose faith. We need people around us who are committed to the same goals. To change our communities, we need to shift entire organizations and institutions. It only takes about 20% of the members of a group to change and then the whole group changes. That's one in five..So, look at five people to your left, and five to your right. It only takes you and one of the other ten to make a change.

The journey is long to rewire our brain, and to reformat our culture. But change can also happen in a heartbeat.

Look into your own heart. Just take a moment to take in who you are. Don't think. Just feel. Just be. Sure, there's some darkness, and maybe, like Marlow, you whisper, "The horror, the horror." But there is also a spacious light, and there is room for others. There is a great deal more kindness than is ever spoken.

The heart knoweth.

ADDITIONAL READINGS

Wikipedia. "Spirituality"

There is no single, widely agreed definition of spirituality. Surveys of the definition of the term, as used in scholarly research, show a broad range of definitions ranging from uni-dimensional definitions, such as a personal belief in a supernatural realm, to broader concepts, such as a quest for an ultimate/sacred meaning transcending the base/material aspects of life, and/or a sense of awe/wonderment and reverence toward the universe. A survey of reviews by McCarroll dealing with the topic of spirituality gave twenty-seven explicit definitions, among which "there was little agreement." This causes some difficulty in trying to study spirituality systematically; i.e., it impedes both understanding and the capacity to communicate findings in a meaningful fashion. Indeed, many of spirituality's core features are not unique to spirituality alone; for example German philosopher Arthur Schopenhauer (a famous atheist) regarded self-transcendence, asceticism and the recognition of one's connection to all as a key to ethical living.

Wikipedia. "Religion"

Religion is a modern Western concept. Parallel concepts are not found in many current and past cultures; there is no equivalent term for "religion" in many languages. Scholars have found it difficult to develop a consistent definition, with some giving up on the possibility of a definition. Others argue that regardless of its definition, it is not appropriate to apply it to non-Western cultures.

An increasing number of scholars have expressed reservations about ever defining the "essence" of religion. They observe that the way we use the concept today is a particularly modern construct that would not have been understood through much of history and in many cultures outside of the West (or even in the West until after the Peace of Westphalia). The MacMillan Encyclopedia of Religions states:

> "The very attempt to define religion, to find some distinctive or possibly unique essence or set of qualities that distinguish the "religious" from the remainder of human life, is primarily a Western concern. The attempt is a natural consequence of the Western speculative, intellectualistic, and scientific disposition. It is also the

product of the dominant Western religious mode, what is called the Judeo-Christian climate or, more accurately, the theistic inheritance from Judaism, Christianity, and Islam. The theistic form of belief in this tradition, even when downgraded culturally, is formative of the dichotomous Western view of religion. That is, the basic structure of theism is essentially a distinction between a transcendent deity and all else, between the creator and his creation, between God and man."

Modern definitions

The anthropologist <u>Clifford Geertz</u> defined religion as a

"[…] system of symbols which acts to establish powerful, pervasive, and long-lasting moods and motivations in men by formulating conceptions of a general order of existence and clothing these conceptions with such an aura of factuality that the moods and motivations seem uniquely realistic.

[…] we have very little idea of how, in empirical terms, this particular miracle is accomplished. We just know that it is done, annually, weekly, daily, for some people almost hourly; and we have an enormous ethnographic literature to demonstrate it."

The theologian <u>Antoine Vergote</u> took the term "supernatural" simply to mean whatever transcends the powers of nature or human agency. He also emphasized the "cultural reality" of religion, which he defined as

"[…] the entirety of the linguistic expressions, emotions and, actions and signs that refer to a supernatural being or supernatural beings."

<u>Peter Mandaville</u> and <u>Paul James</u> intended to get away from the modernist dualisms or dichotomous understandings of immanence/transcendence, spirituality/materialism, and sacredness/secularity. They define religion as

"[…] a relatively-bounded system of beliefs, symbols and practices that addresses the nature of existence, and in which communion with others and Otherness is *lived* as if it both takes in and spiritually transcends socially-grounded ontologies of time, space, embodiment and knowing."

According to the MacMillan Encyclopedia of Religions, there is an experiential aspect to religion which can be found in almost every culture:

"[…] almost every known culture [has] a depth dimension in cultural experiences […] toward some sort of ultimacy and transcendence that will provide norms and power for the rest of life. When more or less distinct patterns of behavior are built around this depth dimension in a culture, this structure constitutes religion in its historically recognizable form. Religion is the organization of life around the depth dimensions of experience – varied in form, completeness, and clarity in accordance with the environing culture."

Wikipedia. "Lived Religion"

Robert Orsi defines lived religion as including "the work of social agents/actors themselves as narrators and interpreters (and reinterpreters) of their own experiences and histories, recognizing that the stories we tell about others exist alongside the many and varied stories they tell of themselves." Orsi understands lived religion to be centered on the actions and interpretations of a religious person.

Wikipedia. "Spiritual but not Religious (SBNR)"

(SBNR) is a popular phrase and initialism used to self-identify a life stance of spirituality that takes issue with organized religion as the sole or most valuable means of furthering spiritual growth. Spirituality places an emphasis upon the well-being of the "mind-body-spirit," so "holistic" activities, such as chi, reiki, and yoga, are common within the SBNR movement. In contrast to religion, spirituality has often been associated with the interior life of the individual.

"Do Animals Have Spiritual Experiences? Yes, They Do" by Mark Bekoff

So, what can we say about animal spirituality? Of course, much turns on how the word "spiritual" is defined, but for the moment let's simply consider nonmaterial, intangible, and introspective experiences as spiritual, of the sort that humans have.

Consider waterfall dances, which are a delight to witness. Sometimes a chimpanzee, usually an adult male, will dance at a waterfall with total abandon. Why? The actions are deliberate but obscure. Could it be they are a joyous response to being alive, or even an expression of the chimp's awe of <u>nature</u>? Where, after all, might human spiritual impulses originate?

<u>Jane Goodall</u> (2005. *Primate spirituality. In The Encyclopedia of Religion and Nature*. edited by B. Taylor. Thoemmes Continuum, New York. Pp. 1303-1306) wonders whether these dances are indicative of religious behavior, precursors of religious ritual. She describes a chimpanzee approaching one of these falls with slightly bristled hair, a sign of heightened arousal. "As he gets closer, and the roar of the falling water gets louder, his pace quickens, his hair becomes fully erect, and upon reaching the stream he may perform a magnificent display close to the foot of the falls. Standing upright, he sways rhythmically from foot to foot, stamping in the shallow, rushing water, picking up and hurling great rocks. Sometimes he climbs up the slender vines that hang down from the trees high above and swings out into the spray of the falling water. This 'waterfall dance' may last ten or fifteen minutes." Chimpanzees also dance at the onset of heavy rains and during violent gusts of wind. Goodall asks, "Is it not possible that these performances are stimulated by feelings akin to wonder and awe? After a waterfall display the performer may sit on a rock, his eyes following the falling water. What is it, this water?"

Goodall wonders, "If the chimpanzee could share his feelings and questions with others, might these wild elemental displays become ritualized into some form of animistic religion? Would they worship the falls, the deluge from the sky, the thunder and lightning — the gods of the elements? So all-powerful; so incomprehensible."

Goodall admits that she'd <u>love</u> to get into their minds even for a few moments. It would be worth years of research to discover what animals see and feel when they look at the stars. In June 2006, Jane and I visited the Mona Foundation's chimpanzee sanctuary near <u>Girona, Spain</u>. We were told that Marco, one of the rescued chimpanzees, does a dance during thunderstorms during which he looks like he is in a trance. Perhaps numerous animals engage in these rituals, but we haven't been lucky enough to see them. Even if they are rare, they are important to note and to study.

"Animals Said to Have Spiritual Experiences"
from *Discovery News*

Animals (not just people) likely have spiritual experiences, according to a prominent neurologist who has analyzed the processes of spiritual sensation for over three decades.

Research suggests that spiritual experiences originate deep within primitive areas of the human brain – areas shared by other animals with brain structures like our own. The trick, of course, lies in proving animals' experiences.

"Since only humans are capable of language that can communicate the richness of spiritual experience, it is unlikely we will ever know with certainty what an animal subjectively experiences," Kevin Nelson, a professor of neurology at the University of Kentucky, told *Discovery News*. "Despite this limitation, it is still reasonable to conclude that since the most primitive areas of our brain happen to be the spiritual, then we can expect that animals are also capable of spiritual experiences," added Nelson, author of the book *The Spiritual Doorway in the Brain*.

"What is Spirituality?"
by Rev. Meredith Garmon

So, what is spirituality? It's a term that encompasses transcendent love, inner peace, "all-right-ness," acceptance, awe, beauty, wonder, humility, gratitude, a freshness of experience; a feeling of plenitude, abundance, and deep simplicity of all things; "the oceanic feeling," Sigmund Freud spoke of, calling it "a sense of indissoluble union with the great All, and of belonging to the universal."

In moments of heightened spiritual experience, the gap between self and world vanishes. The normal experience of time leaves us, and each moment has a quality of the eternal in it. Symptoms of developing spirituality include:

- increased tendency to let things happen rather than make them happen;
- more frequent attacks of smiling from the heart;
- more frequent feelings of being connected with others and nature;
- more frequent episodes of overwhelming appreciation;
- decisions flow more from intention or spontaneity and less from fears based on past experience;
- greater ability to enjoy each moment;
- decreased worrying;
- decreased interest in conflict, in interpreting the actions of others, in judging others, and in judging self;
- increased nonjudgmental curiosity;
- increased capacity to love without expecting anything in return;
- increased receptivity to kindness offered and increased interest in extending kindness to others.

By orienting toward the elevated – whether in compassion, ethics, art, or experience of divine presence – we transcend the ego defense mechanisms by which most of us spend our lives governed.

Psychologist Robert Cloninger and his team at the Center for Well-Being of the Department of Psychiatry of the School of Medicine of Washington University in St. Louis sought a way to define spirituality more definitely, empirically, and measurably. Their 240-item questionnaire called the "Temperament and Character Inventory," includes spirituality (they call it self-transcendence) as one of the dimensions of character. As Cloninger measures it, spirituality is the sum of three subscales: self-forgetfulness, transpersonal identification, and acceptance.

First, self-forgetfulness. This is the proclivity for becoming so immersed in an activity that the boundary between self and other seems to fall away. Whether the activity is sports, painting, playing a musical instrument, we might sometimes lose ourselves in it, and the sense of being a separate independent self takes a vacation.

Second, transpersonal identification. This is recognizing oneself in others – and others in oneself. If you have ever found yourself looking at another person – or another being – with a feeling that you are that other, their body embodies you – or if you have looked at yourself with a sense that your being embodies others – then you have experienced transpersonal identification. Spirituality involves connecting with the world's suffering and apprehending that suffering as our very own.

Transpersonal identification goes beyond "there but for the grace of God go I." It's not that grace saves you from the unfortunate circumstances that others endure. Nothing saves you because, in fact, you are not saved from those circumstances. If anyone is hungry, then you are hungry, for the hungry are you. That's transpersonal identification.

Third, acceptance. This is the ability to accept and affirm reality just as it is, even the hard parts, even the painful and tragic parts. Spiritually mature people are in touch with the suffering of the world, yet also and simultaneously feel joy in that connection. "Acceptance" does not mean complacency about oppression, injustice and harm. Indeed, the spiritually mature are also often the most active and the most effective in working for peace and social justice. They are energized to sustain that work because they can accept reality just as it is, even as they also work to change it. Because they are not attached to results of their work, they avoid debilitating disappointment and burn-out and are able to maintain the work for justice cheerfully. Because they find joy in each present moment, they avoid recrimination and blame. They see that blame merely recapitulates the very reactivity that is at the root of oppression.

Add together your scores for self-forgetfulness, transpersonal identification, and acceptance. The sum is your spirituality score.

Here's the thing, though. It's not a matter of will. It's not a matter of volition. It's not a matter of weighing the pros and cons and making a decision. You can't decide to be more spiritual or more spiritually mature.

If you are low in spirituality – that is, as Cloninger finds, you are practical, self-conscious, materialistic, controlling, characterized by rational objectivity and material success – you can't wake up one morning and decide you are no longer going to be that way. It's who you are, and your own rational objectivity will very sensibly point out to you that you don't even know what it would mean to not be that way.

What you can decide, what is a matter of will and volition, is whether to take up a certain kind of discipline called a spiritual practice – and just see where it takes you. I know that these days all kinds of things get called a spiritual practice. But let's differentiate spiritual practice from just something you do.

Quilting, piano-playing, or hiking might or might not qualify as spiritual practice – that is, might or might not tend to produce the symptoms of developing spirituality. An activity is more likely to work as spiritual practice if you seriously treat it as one.

First, treating a practice as a spiritual practice means engaging the activity with mindfulness – focusing on the activity as you do it, with sharp awareness of each present moment.

Second, treating a practice as a spiritual practice means engaging the activity with intention of thereby cultivating spiritual development – reflecting as you do the activity (or just before and just after) on your intention to manifest those symptoms of spiritual development in your life.

Third, treating a practice as a spiritual practice means sometimes engaging the activity with a group that gathers expressly to do the activity in a way that cultivates spirituality – sharing each other's spiritual reflections before, during, or after doing the activity together.

Fourth – and most of all – it requires establishing a foundation of spiritual openness. There are three basic daily practices for everyone that over time develop a foundation upon which some other practice can grow into a real spiritual practice.

- Silence. 15 minutes a day being still and quiet, just bringing attention to your own amazing breathing.
- Journaling. 15 minutes a day writing about your gratitudes, your highest hopes and your experiences of awe.

- Study. 15 minutes a day reading "wisdom literature" – the essays of Pema Chodron or Thomas Merton, the poems of Rumi or Mary Oliver, the Dao de Jing, the Bible's book of Psalms – just to mention a very few examples of wisdom literature.

With these three daily practices building your foundation of spiritual awareness, then gardening, yoga, or throwing pottery are much better positioned to truly be spiritual practices for you.

Reflection Questions

Don't treat these questions like "homework" or a list that needs to be covered in its entirety. Instead, simply pick the one question that "hooks" you most and let it lead you where you need to go. The goal of these questions is not to help you analyze what spirituality means in the abstract, but to figure out what, if anything, the concept means for you and your daily living. So, which question is calling to you? Which one contains "your work?" You can use these questions for journaling, or to spark conversation with others. For all the readings that are not explicitly multispecies, ask yourself:

a. How is the author addressing or not addressing a multispecies perspective?

b. How would you add to these readings to have them address a multispecies perspective?

c. Do the readings have more meaning to you with or without a multispecies perspective?

1. What is your definition of spirituality?

2. Can you think of a multispecies definition?

3. How do you describe a spiritual practice?

4. Do you have spiritual practices? What are they? Do you wish you practiced more?

5. How have spiritual practices contributed to your life?

6. How have your spiritual practices contributed to other's lives?

7. How might spiritual practices be good for or harmful for other species?

8. How do animals fit into your spiritual practice (are other species part of your spiritual practice)?

9. What is your definition of religion?

10. Can you think of a multispecies definition?

11. Do you see a difference between your definition of spirituality and religion?

12. How might religion be good for or harmful for other species?

13. How do you deal with a heavy or dark heart? How do you lighten or enlighten your heart?

14. What spiritual or religious experiences have you had in our life?

15. What role does community play in your religious or spiritual life?

Weekly Nurture Nature Practices

A. <u>Nurturing Yourself</u>

1. Consider an individual of another species. Perhaps the animal is in your home or near it, or maybe even far away. Imagine yourself being with this being, living out a typical day with them. You as a human are accepted by them and this animal continues their normal daily routine. Now imagine that you are the same species as the animal and are accepted. What do you experience? What do you feel? What needs are met, or unmet?

    Take time to journal your experiences and then ask yourself: How does this experience add to your spirituality? How are you broadened beyond your own daily routine and ego concerns? How are you connected to something larger than yourself? Does your mindfulness, sense of compassion, or big view change?

2. Read all the excerpts in the background readings and then write your own reflection of what role spirituality and religion have in your life. Make a plan for how you can grow and nurture your spiritual intelligence.

3. Go for a spiritual walk where you breathe deeply, looking up and all around, being as observant as you can. If your mind wanders from what you are observing, gently remind yourself to let these thoughts go. When are you are ready (about midway on the walk), repeat this phrase as you walk: "No wonder everything is as it is, for everything is connected in beauty and tragedy."

B. Nurturing Others

1. Ask others about how they see the role of religion and spirituality in the well-being of multiple species and the earth. If they are open to it, offer to them helpful ways to think of spirituality in ways that could help them and other beings.

C. Nurturing Our Communities

1.   Invite others to attend the next gathering of this group.
2. If you belong to a spiritual or religious community, consider holding a discussion or class on this topic.

Resources

Multispecies Perspectives
- Ted Andrews. *Animal-Speak: The Spiritual and Magical Powers of Creatures Great and Small.*
- Mark Bekoff. "Do Animals Have Spiritual Experiences? Yes, they do" https://www.psychologytoday.com/blog/animal-emotions/200911/do-animals-have-spiritual-experiences-yes-they-do
- Jane Goodall. "Primate Spirituality" http://www.religionandnature.com/ern/sample/Goodall--PrimateSpirituality.pdf
- Cara M Gubbins, PhD. *Divine Beings: The Spiritual Lives and Lessons of Animals.*
- Carol Guess and Kelly Magee. *With Animal.*
- Derrick Jensen. *A Language Older than Words.*
- Danielle MacKinnon. *Animal Lessons: Discovering Your Spiritual Connection with Animals.*
- Karleen Strange. *The Spiritual Nature of Animals: A Country Vet Explores the Wisdom, Compassion, and Souls of Animals.*

- Jennifer Viegas. "Animals Said to Have Spiritual Experiences" *Discovery News.* http://www.nbcnews.com/id/39574733/ns/technology_and_science-science/t/animals-said-have-spiritual-experiences/#.XCP-Hc_Yo8Y
- Wikipedia. "Animal Faith" https://en.wikipedia.org/wiki/Animal_faith

General Perspectives
- "Spiritual but not Religious." - https://en.wikipedia.org/wiki/Spiritual_but_not_religious
- Kevin Nelson. "The Spiritual Doorway in the Brain: A Neurologist's Search for the God Experience"

Video
- JP Spears. "How to be Ultraspiritual" https://www.youtube.com/watch?v=1kDso5ElFRg

Guide #8: Freedom and Liberation

Nurture
Nature
Yours, Ours, Theirs, Earth's

Guide #8 Table of Contents

FORMAT FOR NURTURE NATURE COMMUNITY ·152

READINGS:

Main Readings: Interconnected Liberation ·153

Additional Readings ·157

Liberation and Freedom Quotations · 168

REFLECTIONS

Reflection Questions · 171

NURTURE NATURE PRACTICES

Weekly Nurture Nature Practices · 174

Other Suggested Practices · 176

RESOURCES · 177

Published by One Earth Conservation, www.oneearthconservation.org info@oneearthconservation.org

Please help us to continue to provide free resources for the public, such as this guide, by giving a tax-deductible donation to One Earth Conservation at: https://www.oneearthconservation.org/donate All proceeds go to directly to helping the people and the parrots of the world.

Thanks to Rev. Meredith Garmon and Community Unitarian Universalist Congregation (http://www.cucwp.org/) for compiling some of these materials as part of their Journey Group program.

Photo credit: page 179 Christianna Martynowski

Format for Nurture Nature Community

We speak and listen deeply with our hearts and minds, allowing each to speak without interruptions, questions, or advice (unless solicited). The facilitator will help guide us in this so we can make the deepest connections possible to ourselves, others, earth, and earth's beings.

Arriving/Warm Up

As you arrive, make a name tag and draw a picture or write a word representing where you have freedom or liberation, or where you have seen others experiencing these. Share with one another why you drew what you did.

Opening Words

To be free, in a planetary sense, is to feel that you belong to earth. To be free, in a social sense, is to feel at home in a democratic framework. – E.B. White

Check In

Share your name, why you are here today and where you are from. If inclined, share where you yearn for freedom. If your group meets for a longer time, and the group is not large, share what's been happening in your life. How is it with your soul, spirit, mind, body today? (Pause between each sharing for 10 seconds, and have a minute of silence after all sharing.)

Shared Exploration

Review the main readings and have each person briefly suggest an important learning from them that might benefit others (we teach one another).

Our Shared Nurture Nature Practice (Discussion and Reflection)

You are invited to share a story from your own life - a relationship you have with another species (flora or fauna) that offered liberation or freedom for you, or for them. Discuss what these stories and resources in this guide mean to you (to guide reflection – see Reflection Questions).

Our Nurture Nature Practice (Embodiment)

Nurturing Our Spirituality with a Walk

Next Steps

What does your deepening on this theme ask of you to do? Of us together?

Confirm facilitator, location, date/time and subject of next meeting

Check Out

From everything we've shared during this time together, what overall message stands out for you?

What gratitude and affirmation would you like someone else to know?

Closing Words

May you be like a bird in the sky,

knowing how sweet it would be if you found you could fly

Oh, you'd soar to the sun and look down at the sea,

and then you'd sing 'cause you'd know how it feels to be free.

(adapted from Billy Taylor and Dick Dallas's song, "I wish I Knew How It Would Feel To Be Free")

MAIN READINGS

Interconnected Liberation
Rev. Dr. LoraKim Joyner

I believe that none of us can be liberated until all of us are. Our liberation is interconnected, as wisely related to me by Tomás Manzanares, an indigenous leader from the Moskitia region of Honduras. I was visiting his area to witness and stand in solidarity with the villages that wish to resist the overwhelming forces that seek to extract their trees, steal their wild parrots for the illegal wildlife trade, take their land, and impose violence, corruption, and the drug trade as a way of life. Tomás stood up to these forces that were destroying his ancestral lands. For his efforts, he made enemies who ambushed him one day, and he was shot four times. He nearly died. His whole village had to flee because they were likewise threatened with their lives. Yet, four months later he returned to the ghost-like village to work with me and others on parrot conservation. We had to hire a squad of soldiers from the Honduran military to accompany us and keep us safe. I asked him why he was willing to risk his life. He replied, "Doctora, everything is at risk so I am willing to risk everything. If the parrots don't make it, neither do my people."

He knew that for his people to be free, the parrots had to be free too. The freedom of both is severely threatened and curtailed. Freedom is at risk, always, when one has power over another, therefore in our culture of domination we have much work to do to promote freedom, for people, for beings, for all. None of us can be free until all of us are, because we are interconnected to one another. We cannot escape the damage done to the bodies and minds of others, for if we turn away from this reality, we turn away from all reality, and we live disconnected and ever lonelier and less engaged with life on this planet. We must get at the roots of oppression that threaten us all, and this is why we work for mutual liberation and freedom.

This letter from the "Parrot Nation" explains how.

Dear Homo sapiens,

Whoever you are in the Americas, you are tied to the harvesting of parrots. If you claim indigenous blood, you took parrots for food and home long before Europeans ever came ashore. And if you claim European descent, your ancestors started taking parrots from the Americas with the very first return voyage of Christopher Columbus. Those of African descent perhaps captured parrots in their homeland and traded in them as well once in the Americas, especially in the Caribbean. If you are currently in North America, you too have been importing parrots for decades, especially if you are from the USA. You also were part of a national genocide that wiped out not just the indigenous humans, but North America's indigenous parrot, the Carolina parakeet. And if you are a parrot, your genetic background knows of a plentitude of your kind that darkened skies with the size of your flocks, whereas now your diminished size only clouds both human and avian spirit.

Let us not judge one another, for none of us escapes the domination system under which we live. Our cultures taught us well the habits of oppression, white supremacy, racism, colonialism, and speciesism. Whether agent or recipient of a harmful act or thought, both are prisoners in a world less beautiful, more dangerous, and less biodiverse. We have been led to believe that we must sell or extract what is rightfully ours, our native and biological heritage, our children's future and the future of all earth's children, to survive in the oppressor's world.

Every parrot we poach, sell, or home are the pieces of silver that betray our own well-being and that of others. For we are saying that life does not matter, earth does not matter, the future does not matter, I do not matter, and neither do you. You are being bribed with a false sense of connection and security, needs which cannot even remotely be met by a captive parrot alone.

Rise up poachers, lay down your slingshots, machetes, axes, and climbing ropes and spikes. These are all tools of the oppressor, which enslave you as you capture others.

Traders and buyers, empty your pockets of greed, for earth's temple should not be a den of thieves. When you sell a being, you have sold your soul.

You with homed parrots, open up the doors to your caged minds, for when you imprison another, you imprison yourself. Do not take another caged bird into your home, except for a rescue bird, and, care for the ones you already have with every effort you can.

And you parrots, beat your wings against those cage doors until the sounds of the captive's cry can be heard around the world.

Let your lament be the wind upon which we all rise. If one is fallen, so are we all.

Choose liberation. Let us all be free at last.

With Hope for All,
The Parrot Nations

I have worked for liberation for all beings my entire life, and it is so much harder than simply choosing, though that alone requires courage and engagement. Why would any one of us take our heads out of the sand or storm that beach only to take on any more work, stress, guilt, or shame than we already carry? I answer this with my own aching heart (and I suspect yours aches as well), "I believe that on the other side of confession is liberation" (Bryan

Stevenson). So, let us share our stories of how we all are caught in the system of domination, power over, and oppression. We will not compete as to who has more worth depending on our behavior, but we will listen and take the hands, paws, wings, fins, and hooves of all as we strengthen our multispecies communities.

Stevenson goes on, "We are all broken by something. We have all hurt someone and have been hurt. We all share the condition of brokenness even if our brokenness is not equivalent. The ways in which I have been hurt – and have hurt others – are different from the ways Jimmy Dill suffered and caused suffering. But our shared brokenness connected us. But simply punishing the broken – walking away from them or hiding them from sight – only ensures that they remain broken and we do, too." There is no wholeness outside of our connected animality.

I believe that we cannot be free, or free others, until we talk about the brokenness that connects us, until we talk of the abuse and use of ourselves and others in our culture of domination. We must talk of how all lives, and by all, I mean all species, have been harmed or imprisoned by our lack of creative imagination of what freedom would look like for all beings.

A life of freedom is being able to work at your own speed and choice for meeting your needs and to have the resources to choose freely. So many of the animals in our lives and around us do not have these choices. Where can we offer more freedom to the animals in our lives?

I know the tightness in the belly and in the mind when we speak of animal liberation and freedom for others. I recall how Peter Singer's book, "Animal Liberation," has probably caused more arguments than most any other book ever printed. It tied racist and sexist views to actions of discrimination, and how this same process is at work in speciesism, which allows us to think of others, of any species, as having an inferior status. We see them not as individuals, but as objects and means to fulfill our desires. Who really wants the challenge of this task, to either have the conversation with others, or to be shamed or forced into changing our behavior, when we are unsure if anything we do will have any impact?

I say we go forth, the outcome of our pursuit for mutual liberation unknowable. We don't know what such a world would look like, but if we don't look deep into the false girders that build walls to cage our own lives, we won't invite the possibility of what could be. The *adjacent possible*, writes Steven Johnson, "is a kind of shadow future, hovering on the edges of the present state of things, a map of all the ways in which the present can reinvent itself." The past and present prepare us for any number of futures. Depending on what groundwork has been laid and what ideas are floating around, certain new thoughts become thinkable. As Johnson suggests, "The strange and beautiful truth about the adjacent possible is that its boundaries grow as you explore them."

We come together to explore the possible, in freedom, for freedom.

ADDITIONAL READINGS

The Animal's Agenda: Freedom, Compassion, and Coexistence in the Human Age by Mark Bekoff and Jessica Pierce

The essence of ethology of freedom is that behavior is a window onto what animals really want and need – to be free to live their own lives, to be free from the suffering and exploitation to which we subject them – but only if we are looking the right way: straight into the eyes of the animals themselves.

Freedom is the key to many aspects of animal well-being. And lack of freedom is at the root of many of the miseries we intentionally and unintentionally inflict on animals under our "care" – whether they suffer from physical or social isolation, or from being unable to move freely about their world and engage the various senses and capacities for which they are so exquisitely evolved. To do better in our responsibilities toward animals, we must do what we can do to make their freedoms the fundamental needs we promote and protect, even when it means giving those needs priority over some of our own wants.

Real freedom for animals is the one value we don't want to acknowledge, because it would require a deep examination of our own behavior. It might mean we should change the way we treat and relate to animals, not just to make cages bigger or provide new enrichment activities to blunt the sharp edges of boredom and frustration, but to allow animals much more freedom in a wide array of venues.

...Building on the momentum of increased global concern for the well-being of individual animals, we must work toward a future of greater compassion, freedom, and justice for all. This is the right thing to do. The full expression of our humanity demands that we undertake a transition to the "Compassionocene," an era defined by our compassion for other animals. Expanding the meaning and application of the Five Freedoms – liberating them from the welfarist paradigm – will allow us to reassess what exactly it means to respect and enhance the freedom of animals. The welfarist paradigm is when we place the well-being of another species below human wants and needs. We want the animals to live well, but only as it fits into our self-prioritizing of our wants and needs. "Welfare concerns generally focus on prevention or reliving suffering, and making sure animals are being well-fed and cared for, without questioning the underlying conditions of captivity or constraint that shape the very nature of their lives."

What Does Freedom Mean for Animals? (Quotes within *The Animal's Agenda*):

"We have no idea what freedom means. But we can certainly appreciate what the lack of freedom means." – Michael Tobias

"Self-determination. Including the choice of where to roam, fly, swim, choice of friends, choice of activities, choice of food, choice of mates, choice of home/nest, and even poor choices that end their lives, but at least death came in the midst of freedom." – Sarah Bexell

"To be free from bodily and psychological exploitation by humans...to be respected by humans and not objectified." – Jo-Anne McArthur

"An intriguing question. I just returned yesterday from eastern Tibet in search of nonhuman animals. An animal in the wild is free to spend much of its time in search of food or starve, competing for status and mates, and remaining alert to avoid becoming prey. A captive animal is fed well, its social life, if any, confined to cell mates, and, secure from danger, its existence is blunted and banal, its evolutionary force spent, placing it among the living dead." – George Schaller

"The same as for humans. Freedom to meet our basic physical needs, whatever those might be by species and individual – including freedom of movement (bodily liberty): safe and secure from harm from humans (bodily integrity – and this should include freedom from harm to the mind); freedom to love and bond with whom we wish; respect for our choices, and freedom from humiliation and intentional shaming." – Hope Ferdowisian

"We need also, and especially, to think about what freedom means to animals." – Mark Bekoff

The Five Freedoms (What animals want and need)
UK Report of the Technical Committee to Enquire into the Welfare of Animals Kept
Under Intensive Livestock Husbandry Systems.

1. *Freedom from hunger or thirst* by ready access to fresh water and a diet to maintain full health and vigour
2. *Freedom from discomfort* by providing an appropriate environment including shelter and a comfortable resting area
3. *Freedom from pain, injury or disease* by prevention or rapid diagnosis and treatment
4. *Freedom to express (most) normal behaviour* by providing sufficient space, proper facilities and company of the animal's own kind
5. *Freedom from fear and distress* by ensuring conditions and treatment which avoid mental suffering

Problems with the Five Freedoms (Comments by LoraKim Joyner)

The words "Freedom from" in four of the statements above suggests that it is possible to eliminate certain experiences, when we know this is not possible. It also assumes that we humans should be in control of when an individual experiences any of these issues, and that we can be "all knowing" about when and whether an animal should have their experiences. Experiencing discomfort (emotional and physical) is part of life and necessary for the full range of behaviors in an animal.

The goal, then, is not to reduce these experiences, but to balance them against positive affective experiences, which are not captured in the Five Freedoms model. For that we need to consult the Five Domains model (see below).

Though the Five Freedoms model is not adequate, it can by itself remarkably improve an animal's well-being.

"The Five Domains: Extending the 'Five Domains' model for animal welfare assessment to incorporate positive welfare states."
by David Mellor and NJ Beausoleil

Contemporary animal welfare thinking is increasingly emphasizing the promotion of positive states. There is a need for existing assessment frameworks to accommodate this shift in emphasis. This paper describes extensions to the Five Domains model, originally devised

Guide #8: Freedom and Liberation

to assess welfare compromise, that facilitate consideration of positive experiences that may enhance welfare. As originally configured, the model provided a systematic method for identifying compromise in four physical/functional domains (nutrition, environment, health, behaviour) and in one mental domain that reflects the animal's overall welfare state understood in terms of its affective experiences. The specific modifications described here now facilitate additional identification in each domain of experiences animals have which may be accompanied by positive affects that would enhance welfare. It is explained why the grading scale and indices for evaluating welfare compromise necessarily differ from those for assessing welfare enhancement. Also, it is shown that the compromise and enhancement grades can be combined to provide a single informative symbol, the scaled use of which covers the range from severe welfare compromise and no enhancement to no compromise and high-level enhancement. Adapted thus, the Five Domains model facilitates systematic and structured assessment of positive as well as negative welfare-related affects, the circumstances that give rise to them and potential interactions between both types of affect, all of which extend the utility of the model. Moreover, clarification of the extended conceptual framework of the model itself contributes to the growing contextual shift in animal welfare science towards the promotion of positive states whilst continuing to minimize negative states.

Problems with the Five Domains (Comments by LoraKim Joyner)

Because of the scientific rigor required to asses an animal's well-being in this model, many people may not attempt it, or disregard it, because we don't have the current knowledge to really assess an animal's well-being. The science is improving all the time and, in many cases, we know enough to allow this model to be helpful in our relationships with animals.

Also, because the Five Domains model is set up as a scientific endeavor, it can excuse common sense and further understanding by passing it off as scientific objectivity, without doing the human introspective work on how we, with prejudice and subconsciously, place our individual and own species' needs over that of others, biasing our scientific pursuit.

Definitions of Liberation

<u>Etymology</u>: (n) from Latin *liberationem* "a setting or becoming free."
<u>Synonyms</u>: freedom, freeing, setting free, liberty, emancipation, manumission, release,

unchaining, unshackling, extrication, escape, deliverance, salvation, sovereignty, enfranchisement, absolution, disengagement, disenthrallment, redemption, acquittal, discharge.

Definitions of Freedom

Definition from Dictionary.com, based on Random House Dictionary
free (adj) 1. enjoying personal rights or liberty, as a person who is not in slavery: *a land of free people*. 2. pertaining to or reserved for those who enjoy personal liberty: *They were thankful to be living on free soil*. 3. existing under, characterized by, or possessing civil and political liberties that are, as a rule, constitutionally guaranteed by representative government: *the free nations of the world*. 4. enjoying political autonomy, as a people or country not under foreign rule; independent. 5. exempt from external authority, interference, restriction, etc., as a person or one's will, thought, choice, action, etc.; independent; unrestricted. 6. able to do something at will; at liberty: *free to choose*. 7. clear of obstructions or obstacles, as a road or corridor: *The highway is now free of fallen rock*.
freedom (n) 1. the state of being free or at liberty rather than in confinement or under physical restraint: *He won his freedom after a retrial*. 2. exemption from external control, interference, regulation, etc. 3. the power to determine action without restraint. 4. political or national independence. 5. personal liberty, as opposed to bondage or slavery: *a slave who bought his freedom*. 6. exemption from the presence of anything specified (usually followed by from): *freedom from fear*. 7. the absence of or release from ties, obligations, etc.

Etymology: Online Etymology Dictionary
free (adj) Old English *freo* "free, exempt from, not in bondage, acting of one's own will," also "noble; joyful," from Proto-Germanic *frija-* "beloved; not in bondage" from PIE *priy-a-* "dear, beloved," from root *pri-* "to love." The primary Germanic sense seems to have been "beloved, friend, to love;" which in some languages developed also a sense of "free," perhaps from the terms "beloved" or "friend" being applied to the free members of one's clan. Meaning "clear of obstruction" is from mid-13c.; sense of "unrestrained in movement" is from c. 1300; of animals, "loose, at liberty, wild," late 14c. Meaning "liberal, not parsimonious" is from c. 1300. Sense of "characterized by liberty of action or expression" is from 1630s; of art, etc., "not holding strictly to rule or form," from 1813. Of nations, "not subject to foreign rule or to despotism," recorded in English from late 14c.

freedom (n) Old English _freodom_ "power of self-determination, state of free will; emancipation from slavery, deliverance;" Meaning "exemption from arbitrary or despotic control, civil liberty" is from late 14c. Meaning "possession of particular privileges" is from 1570s.

Synonyms: autonomy, liberty, self-determination, ability, flexibility, immunity, opportunity, power, privilege, right, abandon, discretion, indulgence, latitude, laxity, margin, play, prerogative, unrestraint

"O, Freedom!"
by Rev. Meredith Garmon

(How we balance resistance to society based on domination and our own desires...) is about discernment – discerning what resistances and desires we find in our hearts and in our habits, and discerning whether those are really the resistances and desires we want to be active in our lives. We ask ourselves: What have I been resisting that I should surrender to? On the other hand, what have I been complacently allowing that I should begin resisting? What desires have I been following that I should stop following? On the other hand, what desires have I been ignoring that I should start heeding?

The criterion for such _"should"_ questions comes down to liberation. To re-phrase the questions: Have I been resisting my own liberation, resisting taking the steps that would free me? On the other hand, have I been complacent about accepting limitations when resisting them would be liberating? Have I been a slave to my desires? On the other hand, are there truer, deeper desires that would be freeing to pursue?

A little bit of money frees us from the constraints of poverty. Too much money hinders us with protectiveness and reduced empathy -- we get trapped inside our privilege. A little bit of status, beauty, power, education is liberating. Too much can lead to reduced empathy for those with less – a cage that bars us from wider and deeper connection with all of life. Habits, if they are healthy, can free us from the effort of will it takes to start something, and free up energy for other things. If too much of our action is simply habitual, then habit becomes our prison.

Liberation is always liberation _from_ something: a slave master, prison bars, an addiction, a habit, mental illness, fear, poverty, wealth, other people's expectations, our own expectations, what we think we know. To be liberated from everything would be to become at last fully and completely ourselves – fearless, flowing, infinitely creative, every moment fresh.

Guide #8: Freedom and Liberation

"Freedom, the Half-Won Blessing"
by Rev. Meredith Garmon

In parts of the world, full-scale slavery is still going on. If you're reading this, then chances are that you are not enslaved in that full-scale way and never have been. Even so, I would guess that there has been a metaphorical land of Egypt in your past in which you were bound and from which you now are free.

Yet freedom is the half-won blessing. Modern pharaohs live unchallenged. Chains still there are to break, metal or subtle-made. Resentments, small or large, bind us. A further Exodus awaits us still. And further truth, bright as a burning bush, cries to become known.

We (we who are not under an unrelenting grind of oppression, nor consumed wholly with mere survival) stand midway between full-scale slavery and full-scale liberation. The unfinished work of freedom lies before us.

The first half of freedom is straightforward and negative: no slavery, no masters or overlords, no chains. The second half is paradoxical. We arrive at liberation by accepting the constraints of discipline, by surrendering. By letting go and giving up, we gain. The first half involves being able to do what you want. But then you can become enslaved to your own impulsive wants. So, the second half involves liberating the true self from the bondage of the desiring self.

"Political: Positive and Negative Freedom"
by Rev. Meredith Garmon

A government that protects and ensures the freedom of its citizens must attend to both "negative freedom" and "positive freedom" – concepts from Isaiah Berlin's "Two Concepts of Liberty" (originally a lecture he gave in 1958). Negative freedom is an absence of coercion or interference from others – it's being left alone. The freedoms of our first amendment, for instance, – freedoms of press, speech, religion, and assembly – are negative freedoms, defined by *absence*.

Positive freedom is having the capacity and tools for constructing a life of meaning and purpose – a life not dictated from a single authority but emerging from each individual's unique mix of influences and predispositions.

The more that government, or any authority, makes actions either mandatory or prohibited, the more your negative freedom is limited. Positive freedom is limited when the capacity and tools for constructing meaning and purpose in life are limited. Education, libraries, intellectual property protections, access to markets and channels of communication provide us with the freedom to envision and pursue life projects. Without this positive freedom to pursue purposes of our own choosing, then merely being left unconstrained wouldn't be worth much. On the other hand, without the negative freedom – the relative absence of constraint so that we can pursue those purposes – then positive freedom isn't good for much.

One aspect of positive freedom is self-mastery. If you're subject to every passing whim and impulse, you aren't able to construct a life of much purpose and meaning. You are slave to your own impulses, and aren't free. Another aspect of positive freedom is collaborating with others. A life of meaning and purpose is not solitary, but embedded in relationship. Having a role in your government – participating with others in the creation and regulation of our shared form of life – is thus an essential positive freedom.

Abuses. Positive freedom may be susceptible to abuse from governments seeking to justify paternalism as providing meaning and purpose of citizen's lives. Education then is indoctrinating rather than empowering. Governments may also abuse negative liberty, not only with too many prohibitions and requirements, but also by failing to constrain their citizens from imposing on other citizens. There must be limits on your freedom to limit my freedom.

"Philosophical: Free Will vs. Determinism"
by Rev. Meredith Garmon

Determinism is the claim that everything is caused, and happens the way it happens because of its various causes. If freedom means you get to do what you want, where does your wanting come from? Some combination of genetic predispositions and environmental influences produced the want. You get to choose, but you don't choose the factors that will cause you to choose the way you do. Everything is the product of causes.

Determinism makes a very logical point. Everything that happens is either the product of causal conditions and forces, or it isn't. If it is, then it's not free. If it isn't, then it's random, and randomness isn't free either. (If you saw somebody moving about randomly – muscles contracting here and there without cause or reason – we wouldn't say she was free. Quite the opposite. We'd say she was in the grip of – enslaved by – some bizarre and horrible neurological condition.) "Free will," then, is an incoherent concept.

This logical point is sound, but the sort of free will that is thereby defeated is not the sort of free will that we care about. The freedom we care about is liberation from some force or condition. It might be a slave master or prison bars or an addiction or bad habit or mental illness or poverty. Someone yearning for freedom isn't looking to become uncaused. They want to be guided by purposes that make sense and are rewarding (positive freedom) and they want *not* to be constrained by someone else's commands and threats of painful punishment (negative freedom).

Responsibility. If determinism is true, can we hold people responsible for what they do? Yes. Holding people responsible is a social practice of moral (dis)approval. Moral disapproval sometimes works, so we should keep it. Most of us don't shout profanity at particularly inappropriate times – because the moral disapproval of those around us has taught us not to do that. Moral disapproval, however, doesn't work on people with Tourette's syndrome. We say they aren't responsible for what they do – and what "not responsible" boils down to is that the social practices of praise, blame, censure, and punishment are ineffective causal forces for making them change that behavior.

Much of the time, though, holding people responsible through use of moral language works just fine. If your teenager has misbehaved and protests that causes "made" him do it, you can just reply, "Of course. And now let's see if being grounded will cause better behavior in the future."

The Experience of Freedom. The important question isn't, "Are your actions determined?" The important question is, "What is freedom actually experienced as?" We don't experience freedom as uncaused action, so when the determinist points out that there is no uncaused action, this fact is irrelevant to the experience we're talking about.

One: We experience freedom when one of the causes is a shared language of moral deliberation. When an action happens reflexively or habitually or driven by obsessive-compulsive tendency or by any other mental disorder, we don't experience it as being as free as we do when the language of moral deliberation can play out in our minds and when there's a real possibility that we will carry out the conclusion of that deliberation.

When we say that depression, schizophrenia, and mania aren't free choices, we're saying that talking – at least the language of praise, blame, threats, and ostracism – doesn't do much good. We experience freedom not when our action is uncaused, but when language – particularly the language of moral deliberation – plays a key causal role.

Two: We also experience greater freedom when all our tastes and preferences – howsoever unchosen those tastes and preferences are – are allowed at the table. We don't, in the end, have to act to satisfy every taste, but not squelching or suppressing or denying that we do have the preferences we have is a piece of the experience of freedom.

Three: We experience greater freedom when the causes that are coming from our own body, including our brain, are within the range of normal and healthy, rather than including mental or physical illness.

Long Walk to Freedom (Excerpt)
by Nelson Mandela

It was during those long and lonely years that my hunger for the freedom of my own people became a hunger for the freedom of all people…the oppressor must be liberated just as surely as the oppressed. One who takes away another's freedom is a prisoner of hatred, locked behind the bars of prejudice and narrow mindedness. I am not truly free if I am taking away someone else's freedom, just as surely as I am not free when my freedom is taken from me. The oppressed and the oppressor alike are robbed of their humanity. The truth is we are not yet free; we have merely achieved the freedom to be free, the right not to be oppressed. For to be free is not merely to cast off one's chains but to live in a way that respects and enhances the freedom of others. That is the true test of our devotion to freedom. With freedom comes responsibilities.

"Liberation Is Costly"
by Desmond Tutu

Liberation is costly. Even after the Lord had delivered the Israelites from Egypt, they had to travel through the desert. They had to bear the responsibilities and difficulties of freedom.

There was starvation and thirst and they kept complaining. They complained that their diet was monotonous. Many of them preferred the days of bondage and the fleshpots of Egypt.

We must remember that liberation is costly. It needs unity. We must hold hands and refuse to be divided. We must be ready.

Some of us will not see the day of our liberation physically. But those people will have contributed to the struggle. Let us be united, let us be filled with hope, let us be those who respect one another.

"Alice Walker's 7 Simple Steps to Being a Love Activist"
By Kelle Walsh

From the deck of the "Freedom Flotilla" destined for the Gaza Strip, to standing on the frontlines of healing America's own violent history, author and activist Alice Walker has been a voice for peace for nearly 40 years. She shares the keys to being a LOVE Activist passionately committed to healing our troubled world through peace and an open heart.

1) *Recommit Every Day.* When you're on a mission of peace, your commitment to nonviolence is tested daily. So every day, you're called to recommit to who you are, to keep your heart open and to stand your ground as a peacemaker.

2) *Protect What Matters Most.* Know what you're defending: What's within you that's worth protecting so you don't become just like the people who are trying stop you? Guard it dearly and use it as your inspiration for nonviolence.

3) *Embrace Your Joy.* Peace is not just the cessation of war. It's also the act of embracing JOY. To have peace is to be fully awake and vibrantly alive! Find the small joys in daily acts of peace.

4) *Stand for Truth.* When you stand with, and for, the marginalized and abused, bring a kind heart, an open mind and a good conscience. This can only be achieved by acknowledging what has truly happened. The suffering must be seen and the wounded must be embraced.

5) *Be Courageous.* Women in particular have a key role to play in bringing peace into our homes, communities, spiritual circles and world. So be courageous, even audacious, speak up and share your unique gifts. The world needs your leadership!

6) *Spread Forgiveness.* When you forgive, others feel it deeply. Alice loves the Tonglen practice of breathing in pain and disaster as far as you can, and breathing out peace, prosperity and joy, spreading these good feelings out into the world.

Guide #8: Freedom and Liberation

7) *Love the Earth*. Nature is a vital life-giving source that we cannot take for granted. Be a conscious steward of the Earth. Treat Her with respect and nature will keep us happy and healthy in return.

Liberation and Freedom Quotations

Which of these quotations calls to you? How might you tweak it or them to include species other than humans, or all of life?

Liberation

"We are not trapped or locked up in these bones. No, no. We are free to change. And love changes us. And if we can love one another, we can break open the sky." – Walter Mosley

"No one can be perfectly free until all are free". – Herbert Spencer

"If you have come to help me, you are wasting your time, but if you have come because your liberation is bound up with mine, then let us work together." – Lila Watson

"It is only through disruptions and confusion that we grow and are set free, jarred out of ourselves by the collision of someone else's private world with our own." – Joyce Carol Oates

"I went to the woods because I wished to live deliberately, to front only the essential facts of life, and see if I could not learn what it had to teach, and not, when I came to die, discover that I had not lived." – Henry David Thoreau

"We will find the key to our liberation only when we accept that what we once did to survive is now destroying us." – Laura van Dernoot Lipsky

"When personal guilt in relation to a past event becomes a continuous cloud over your life, you are locked in a mental prison. You have become your own jailer. Although you should not erase your responsibility for the past, when you make the past your jailer, you destroy your future. It is such a great moment of liberation when you learn to forgive yourself, let the burden go, and walk out into a new path of promise and possibility. Self-compassion is a wonderful gift to give yourself." – John O'Donohue

"Comfort...was the key ingredient to making the prisoner crave the prison." – Ashim Shanker

"True wisdom comes in understanding that sometimes, you are both the prison and the key." – Johnathan Jena

"Leaders who do not act dialogically, but insist on imposing their decisions, do not organize the people – they manipulate them. They do not liberate, nor are they liberated: they oppress." – Paulo Freire

"People get used to anything. The less you think about your oppression, the more your tolerance for it grows. After a while, people just think oppression is the normal state of things. But to become free, you have to be acutely aware of being a slave." – Assata Shakur

"Humanity is not without answers or solutions regarding how to liberate itself from scenarios that invariably end with mass exterminations. Tools such as compassion, trust, empathy, love, and ethical discernment are already in our possession. The next sensible step would be to use them." – Aberjhani

"When I look at a block of marble, I see the sculpture inside it. All I have to do is remove what doesn't belong." – Michelangelo

"When things are taking their ordinary course, it is hard to remember what matters." – Marilynne Robinson

"Perhaps, there is no such person who can be called truly free, but only those who can be deemed so by comparison." – Ashim Shanker

Freedom

"Freedom is actually a bigger game than power. Power is about what you can control. Freedom is about what you can unleash." – Harriet Rubin

"A friend is someone who gives you total freedom to be yourself." – Jim Morrison

"Nobody can give you freedom. Nobody can give you equality or justice or anything. If you're a man, you take it." – Malcolm X

"Freedom is not something that anybody can be given. Freedom is something people take, and people are as free as they want to be." – James Baldwin

"The secret to happiness is freedom, and the secret to freedom is courage." – Thucydides

"Instead of trying to make your life perfect, give yourself the freedom to make it an adventure, and go ever upward." – Drew Houston

"Education is the key to unlock the golden door of freedom." – George Washington Carver

"The only way to deal with an unfree world is to become so absolutely free that your very existence is an act of rebellion." – Albert Camus

"A freedom which only asks what's in it for me, a freedom without a commitment to others, a freedom without love or charity or duty or patriotism, is unworthy of our founding ideals, and those who died in their defense." – Barack Obama

"Freedom is what you do with what's been done to you." – Jean-Paul Sartre

"I would like to be remembered as a person who wanted to be free so other people would be also free." – Rosa Parks

"Love does not claim possession, but gives freedom." – Rabindranath Tagore

"I am not free while any woman is unfree, even when her shackles are very different from my own. And I am not free as long as one person of Color remains chained. Nor is any one of you." – Audre Lorde

"Letting go gives us freedom, and freedom is the only condition for happiness. If, in our heart, we still cling to anything – anger, anxiety, or possessions – we cannot be free." – Thích Nhất Hạnh

"Freedom makes a huge requirement of every human being. With freedom comes responsibility. For the person who is unwilling to grow up, the person who does not want to carry his own weight, this is a frightening prospect." – Eleanor Roosevelt

"There can be no real freedom without the freedom to fail." – Eric Hoffer

"To be free, in a planetary sense, is to feel that you belong to earth. To be free, in a social sense, is to feel at home in a democratic framework." – E.B. White

"The last of the human freedoms is to choose one's attitude in any given set of circumstances." – Viktor Frankl

"You can only protect your liberties in this world by protecting the other man's freedom. You can only be free if I am free." – Clarence Darrow

Reflection Questions

Don't treat these questions like "homework" or a list that needs to be covered in its entirety. Instead, simply pick the one question that "hooks" you most and let it lead you where you need to go. The goal of these questions is not to help you analyze what freedom or liberation means in the abstract, but to figure out what, if anything, the concept means for you and your daily living. So, which question is calling to you? Which one contains "your work?" You can use these questions for journaling, or to spark conversations with others. For all the readings that are not explicitly multispecies, ask yourself:
   a. How is the author addressing or not addressing a multispecies perspective?
   b. How would you add to these readings to have them address a multispecies perspective?
   c. Do the readings have more meaning to you with or without a multispecies perspective?

Specific Multispecies Questions:

1.   What does liberation or freedom look for a nonhuman species? How possible is it for other species to experience freedom and liberation?

2.   Are there differences between species for defining or experiencing freedom and liberation?

3.   What are the causes that diminish freedom and liberation in our own species and others? How might these causes be related?

4.   How are you called to work towards liberation for yourself, and for life on earth? What holds you back from this liberating work?

General Questions on Liberation:

1.   How liberated is it possible for a human being to be? How liberated are you?

2.   What are your chains?

3.   Have you let yourself become imprisoned by the fear of missing out? By the imaginings of what might have been or what others have?

4.   "When things are taking their ordinary course, it is hard to remember what matters." (Marilynne Robinson) Do you need to liberate yourself from the ordinary?

5.   Is the thing you do to feel better actually making you feel worse? Has what you turn to for liberation become a bit of a trap?

6.   "It's very simple. When I look at a block of marble, I see the sculpture inside it. All I have to do is remove what doesn't belong." (Michelangelo's reply after he was asked how he could create such beautiful works). What can you remove that doesn't belong in yourself? What might be liberated by removing what doesn't belong? What beauty is waiting for you to give it a bit more room?

7.   Is it time to forgive (and free) yourself?

8.   Are you ready to take off the mask? Do you even notice that it is on?

9.   What is the relationship between liberation and creativity? Does liberation facilitate creativity? Does creativity facilitate liberation?

10. How liberated is it possible for a society to be? How liberated is ours?

11. What is the relationship between your personal liberation and your society's liberation?

12. "If you have come to help me, you are wasting your time, but if you have come because your liberation is bound up with mine, then let us work together." (Lila Watson). Have your efforts to help others fully recognized that your own liberation is bound up with theirs?

13. Are you looking for liberation and freedom in faraway places and possibly not noticing they are waiting for you right back at home? Or they are right there where you are standing now?

14. Is kindness waiting for you to pick it up and liberate someone? Maybe even yourself?

General Questions on Freedom:

1. What is freedom? (What does freedom mean to you?)

2. "Freedom is actually a bigger game than power. Power is about what you can control. Freedom is about what you can unleash." (Harriet Rubin) What have you used your freedom to unleash?

3. Are you trapped in the escape from pain? All of us have pain. All of us want to escape it. And yet sometimes that effort to escape becomes a prison of its own. What do you do to escape from emotional pain? Drink or eat too much? Keep yourself ridiculously busy?

4. When have you been freed by love?

5. When was quitting an act of freedom for you?

6. Would living more simply bring you freedom?

7. Do you need to laugh your way into freedom? Would laughing at yourself or at what life has dumped in your lap be your way out?

8. Has money increased or decreased your freedom? How would doing something with your wallet make you feel freer?

9. Has age left you feeling more or less free?

10. Are you trapped by your inability to forgive?

11. "I have an instinct that tells me that I am less free when I am living for myself alone." (Thomas Merton) Is living for yourself making you less free?

12. In what ways have you found freedom and responsibility to be connected? Does the prospect of increased responsibility feel like more freedom, or less? Does the prospect of increased freedom feel like more responsibility, or less?

13. What freedom is most important to you? For what freedom are you most grateful?

14. What do you do to promote greater freedom in the world?

15. If determinism were true, would it matter?

16. Is there an area in your life where you don't feel free? What, if anything, do you feel you could do to change that?

17. What is your question about freedom or liberation?

Weekly Nurture Nature Practices

A. Nurture Yourself

There are some things we can never escape even if we want to: a diagnosis, a loss, the responsibility of caregiving, regret, worry, the draining busyness of daily life, the joy-filled but nonstop responsibility of parenting. Some of these burdens are extraordinary; some are routine. But regardless of their weight or intensity, we find ourselves longing for a reprieve. A spiritual timeout. A temporary moment of renewal that lets us feel carefree just long enough to be refilled or to gain a new perspective.

That's what this spiritual exercise is all about: Find a way to feel carefree! Find a way to step outside the weight of whatever you're carrying – even if only for a moment or a day.

To be specific, here is your task:

1. Find a moment of quiet and watch this video-all the way through! https://www.youtube.com/watch?v=pMWU8dEKwXw (Or, at YouTube, search "if only for a second")
2. Spend some time identifying the burden, weight or responsibility from which you need (or would just like) a brief time of escape.
3. Then do something to give you that escape. Do something that leaves you feeling carefree!
4. Come back to your group prepared to share the gift that this moment of freedom gave you.

B. Nurture Others

I. Sometimes it's not us that need a moment of escape, but someone we care about. Stepping away, renewing oneself, taking a break are not gifts that some people are good at giving themselves. Sometimes they need a friend to give it to them or make them do it. So maybe life is calling you to help them escape.

If so, here is your task:

1. Find a moment of quiet and watch this video-all the way through! https://www.youtube.com/watch?v=pMWU8dEKwXw (Or, at YouTube, search "if only for a second")
2. Spend some time identifying someone in your circle of concern that is carrying a burden, weight or responsibility from which they need a brief time of escape. Choose another species if possible.
3. Then do something to give them that gift, to leave them feeling carefree. You can be direct about it or sneaky. Sometimes gifts like these require a surprise or even anonymity.

It might be important for you to drag them into it. Then again, it might be important for them to never know you are behind it. Your assignment is simply to orchestrate it, to make it happen.

4. Come back to your group prepared to share the gift that this moment of freedom gave them – and you.

II. Investigate another species and how their needs are being met in their situation. How is this individual of another species "imprisoned?" How might you liberate them? Consider options and then enact one multispecies act of liberation this week.

3. Nurturing Our Communities is Nurturing Yourself

The task of creating a society in which none are oppressed and all are liberated is demanding and often discouraging work. Keeping ourselves liberated from getting dragged down or burnt out from activism is an essential part of liberating all beings.

Read the article above by Kelle Walsh, "Alice Walker's 7 Simple Steps to Being a Love Activist." In that article, Walsh reports on Walker's 7 steps: 1) Recommit Every Day; 2) Protect What Matters Most; 3) Embrace Your Joy; 4) Stand for Truth; 5) Be Courageous; 6) Spread Forgiveness; 7) Love the Earth.

What do you need to liberate from within you in order to remain engaged in the wider work of liberation? From Walker's list, choose the one that calls to you the most. Once you have your answer, take some time this month to enact that step with a human species and with another species.

Other Suggested Practices

1. Read all the excerpts in the background readings and then write your own reflection of what role freedom and liberation have in your life. Make a plan for how you can grow your nurturing practice of freedom and liberation.

2. Invite others to attend the next gathering of this group.

3. Join with others to work toward liberation for all – perhaps by joining a group oriented towards social justice, liberation, and freedom for more than one oppressed group, such as working to help companion animals or homeless people.

Resources

Multispecies Perspectives

- Marc Bekoff and Jessica Pierce. *The Animals Agenda: Freedom, compassion, and coexistence in the human age.*
- Peter Singer. *Animal Liberation: The Definitive Classic of the Animal Movement.*

Videos and Podcasts

- *The Exodus Story and the Necessity of Desire for Liberation.* http://www.onbeing.org/blog/exodus-story-and-necessity-desire-liberation/3840
- *Liberation as Harmony with Nature and Another Person.* https://www.facebook.com/morgan.burks.92/videos/10153769033350630/
- *Liberation through Art: Beyonce's Visionary Fiction – Formation.* http://tinyurl.com/gtclrvd
- *Somewhere in America.* A liberation poem performed by three young women who bravely speak unspoken truths that are all too often silenced. https://www.youtube.com/watch?v=cD6UrVHNRMc

TED Talks on Freedom:

- Judson Brewer. *A Simple Way to Break a Bad Habit.* http://www.ted.com/talks/judson_brewer_a_simple_way_to_break_a_bad_habit
- Heather Brooke. *Freedom of Information: Citizen Freedom, Government Accountability.* https://www.ted.com/talks/heather_brooke_my_battle_to_expose_government_corruption
- Ruth Chang. *How to Make Hard Choices.* https://www.ted.com/talks/ruth_chang_how_to_make_hard_choices
- Trevor Timm. *Our Free Press, Becoming Less Free.* https://www.ted.com/talks/trevor_timm_how_free_is_our_freedom_of_the_press
- Anthony D. Romero. *Civil Liberties: What Democracy Looks Like.* https://www.ted.com/talks/anthony_d_romero_this_is_what_democracy_looks_like
- Manal al-Sharif. *Heroes for Freedom: A Saudi Woman Who Dared to Drive.* https://www.ted.com/talks/manal_al_sharif_a_saudi_woman_who_dared_to_drive

Books, Articles and Online Information

- Cami Applequist. "Hearing the Right Voices." http://www.uuworld.org/articles/hearing-right-voices

- The Rev. Dr. William J. Barber II and Jonathan Wilson-Hartgrove. *The Third Reconstruction: Moral Mondays, Fusion Politics, and the Rise of a New Justice Movement.* http://www.beacon.org/The-Third-Reconstruction-P1139.aspx
- Tony Campolo. "What is Liberation Theology?" http://www.faithstreet.com/onfaith/2008/04/30/what-is-liberation-theology/3419
- TJ Dawe. "Why Tom Waits Quit Drinking" by TJ Dawe. http://beamsandstruts.com/bits-a-pieces/item/882-the-piano-has-been-drinking-ginger-ale
- Leah Gunning Francis. *Ferguson and Faith: Sparking Leadership and Awakening Community.* http://tinyurl.com/j9o7rcj
- List of Books for Children and Families. http://amzn.com/w/2GSMSOW14MGXP
- Martin Kelley. *The 1965 murder of James Reeb.* http://www.quakerranter.org/2015/03/nytimes-video-remembers-the-1965-selma-james-reeb-attack/
- Mark Ludwig, Editor. *Liberation: New Works on Freedom from Internationally Renowned Poets.* http://www.beacon.org/Liberation-P1146.aspx
- Maria Popova. *Missing Out: Liberating ourselves from the curse of our unlived lives.* https://www.brainpickings.org/2015/08/17/missing-out-adam-phillips/
- Bryan Stevenson. *Just Mercy: A story of justice and redemption.*
- Jim Yardley and Simon Romero. "Pope's Focus on Poor Revives Scorned Theology." http://www.nytimes.com/2015/05/24/world/europe/popes-focus-on-poor-revives-scorned-theology.html

Movies

- *The Shawshank Redemption.* http://www.rottentomatoes.com/m/shawshank_redemption/
- *Harry Potter and the Chamber of Secrets.* The theme of liberation is an undercurrent throughout the Harry Potter series; it is vividly illustrated throughout *Chamber of Secrets,* especially in the story of Dobby the house elf. http://www.imdb.com/title/tt0295297/
- *Romero.* The life and work of Archbishop Oscar Romero who opposed, at great personal risk, the tyrannical repression in El Salvador. http://www.imdb.com/title/tt0098219/
- *Munyurangabo (Liberation Day).* Two friends in Rwanda dealing with the fallout from the genocide which lingers in their consciousness and souls (with subtitles). http://www.spiritualityandpractice.com/films/reviews/view/17972/liberation-day-munyurangabo

- A list of ten movies about women's liberation and feminism (March is Women's History month). http://nonfics.com/10-great-womens-history-films-watch-month/

Songs

- Ledisi. "Take My Hand, Precious Lord" from the *Selma* movie soundtrack. https://www.youtube.com/watch?v=qxVpHiyT5kE
- Beyonce. "Formation." http://adriennemareebrown.net/2016/02/07/beyonces-visionary-fiction-formation/
- David Bowie. "Pressure." https://www.youtube.com/watch?v=YoDh_gHDvkk
- The Bengsons. "Lift Me." https://www.youtube.com/watch?v=X9262w6umIM
- The Bleachers. "I Wanna Get Better." https://www.youtube.com/watch?v=khPf88uxyFo

Liberation in Nicaragua of a wild rescued juvenile
yellow-naped amazon, which is a threatened species of parrot.

Guide #8: Freedom and Liberation

Appendices

Plutchik's Wheel of Emotions · 181

Universal Needs · 182

Five Intelligences Graphic · 183

Multispecies Intelligence Primer · 184

Wild Walks Guide · 186

One Earth Conservation · 188

The Authors · 189

Plutchik's Wheel of Emotions

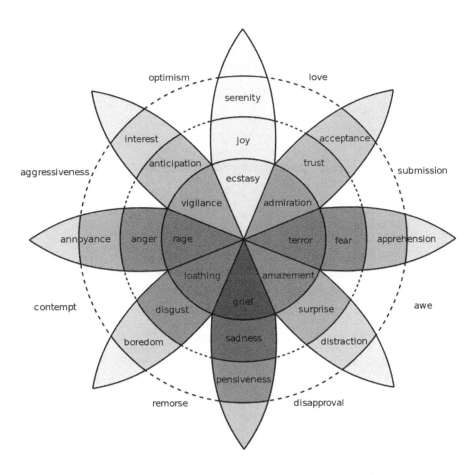

(https://positivepsychologyprogram.com/emotion-wheel/)

Appendices

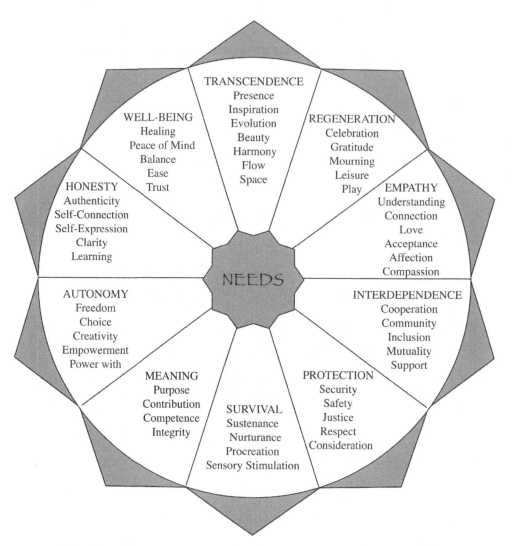

TRANSCENDENCE
Presence
Inspiration
Evolution
Beauty
Harmony
Flow
Space

WELL-BEING
Healing
Peace of Mind
Balance
Ease
Trust

REGENERATION
Celebration
Gratitude
Mourning
Leisure
Play

HONESTY
Authenticity
Self-Connection
Self-Expression
Clarity
Learning

EMPATHY
Understanding
Connection
Love
Acceptance
Affection
Compassion

NEEDS

AUTONOMY
Freedom
Choice
Creativity
Empowerment
Power with

INTERDEPENDENCE
Cooperation
Community
Inclusion
Mutuality
Support

MEANING
Purpose
Contribution
Competence
Integrity

SURVIVAL
Sustenance
Nurturance
Procreation
Sensory Stimulation

PROTECTION
Security
Safety
Justice
Respect
Consideration

Needs: Resources required to sustain and enrich life.
Needs are universal.
Needs make no reference to any specific person
doing any specific thing.

Key Distinction: Need vs. Strategy

Inspired by the work of Marshall Rosenberg, Ph.D. and Manfred Max-Neef, Ph. D.,Chilean economist
© 2005 peaceworks Jim & Jori Manske, CNVC Certified Trainers in Nonviolent Communication[sm]
cnvc.org   radicalcompassion.com

Five Intelligences

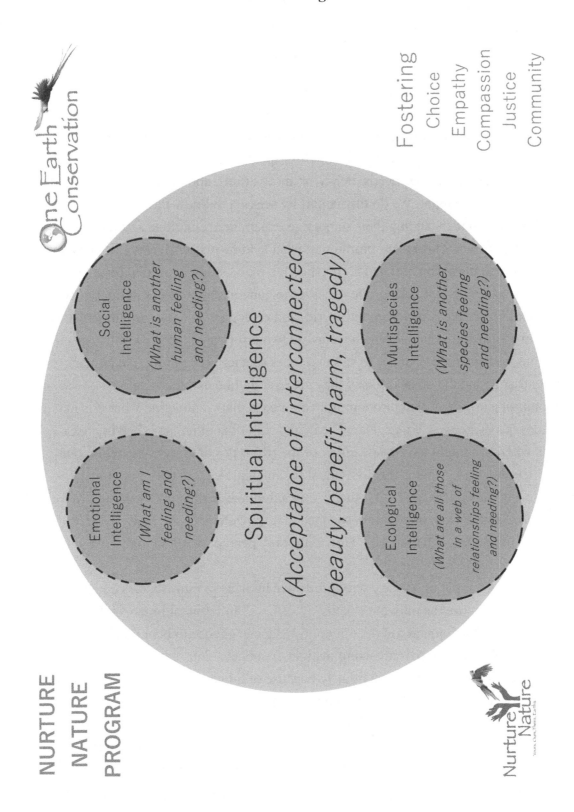

One Earth Conservation

Fostering
Choice
Empathy
Compassion
Justice
Community

Social Intelligence
(What is another human feeling and needing?)

Emotional Intelligence
(What am I feeling and needing?)

Spiritual Intelligence
(Acceptance of interconnected beauty, benefit, harm, tragedy)

Multispecies Intelligence
(What is another species feeling and needing?)

Ecological Intelligence
(What are all those in a web of relationships feeling and needing?)

NURTURE NATURE PROGRAM

Nurture Nature

Multispecies Intelligence Primer

We seek to understand animal nature, ours and others, because we cannot love human nature until we love animal nature.

We humans are prone to judge others as being different, wrong, or of less worth than us. One check to this "othering" and inherent tribalism, is to develop our multispecies intelligence. Multispecies intelligence is the ability to understand and use emotional intelligence, communication, and behavior across species lines for the mutual benefit of all. It requires understanding species needs, behavior, motivations, and interconnecting relations with others and their habitat. We do this in part by seeking to know the motivations for the behaviors, such as understanding their subjective experience (emotions and internal processing) and needs. This means employing what is known as critical anthropomorphism: "Critical anthropomorphism" refers to a perspective in the study of animal behavior that encompasses using the sentience of the observer to generate hypotheses in light of scientific knowledge of the species, its perceptual world, and ecological and evolutionary history. By engaging in critical anthropomorphism we avoid two errors on either end of the spectrum of multispecies understanding: one is to say that other species are nothing like humans (anthrocentrism), and the other is to say they are exactly like us (uncritical anthropomorphism). Critical anthropomorphism means that we imagine what it is like to be in the shoes, paws, hooves, wings, claws, feet, and skin of another, and then to check ourselves where we might have made either of the two types of errors. We put on our scientific lens, and ask, what is this individual feeling and needing? We put on our empathetic, embodied lens, and ask, what is this individual feeling and needing? We employ all the science and sensory and body resonance that is available to us, study, reflect, discuss, check our assumptions, and then ask: How might my perception of another lead to more harm than good?

A prime example of how we wrongfully see humans in multispecies community is the statement, "Humans are the only ones who _____." In terms of prosocial behavior, I have heard it said that humans are the only ones who can choose to beneficially act on another's behalf. Other animals are using instinct or subconscious automatic behavior patterns. Perhaps they are only acting thusly because of human intervention. If ever you are tempted to say "only humans do X," or "humans have greater choice or do similar behaviors for different reasons," or if you read, "what sets humans apart from animals" become immediately suspicious of why you or others are saying that. You ask yourself if such a phrase is to promote human exceptionalism, where humans are better than other animals. There is another kind of human exceptionalism: where humans aren't better than others because of behaviors and intent, but are actually worse. Either way we are committing multispecies errors, distancing ourselves from ourselves and others, and setting up harm to others, and inviting despair, depression, and debilitating disconnection that disempowers us.

In every situation, ask what that particular individual animal is feeling and needing. Use your body, intuition, science, experience, and research to answer this question.

Wild Walks
One Earth Conservation's Nurture Nature Program

Yours, Ours, Theirs, Earth's

Definitions

Emotional Intelligence – the ability to identify, assess, accept, and have choice around our feelings and needs

Social Intelligence – the ability to identify, assess, accept, and have awareness of and connection to others, thus having choice about how to interact so as to create healthy and productive relationships

Multispecies Intelligence – the ability to understand and use emotional and social intelligence, communication, and behavior observation across species lines for the mutual benefit of all

Ecological Intelligence – the capacity to recognize the often-hidden web of connections between individuals of different species and between species' and nature's systems so that humans many minimize harm and maximize flourishing for all

Spiritual Intelligence – the ability to transcend individual ego concerns' and perspective by connecting to that which is greater than self, fostering wisdom, acceptance, compassion, presence, and mindfulness

Our Natural Intelligence   Invites Us To....

Emotional Intelligence ⟶ Be with Yourself in Beauty (Ask, what am I feeling and needing?)

Social Intelligence ⟶ Be with the Other Human in Beauty (Ask, what is another human feeling and needing?)

Multispecies Intelligence ⟶ Be with the Other Species in Beauty (As, what is another species feeling and needing?)

Ecological Intelligence ⟶ Be with all Relationships in Beauty (Ask, what are all those in the web of relationships feeling and needing?)

Spiritual Intelligence ⟶ Be with All in Beauty (Acceptance of interconnected beauty, benefit, harm, tragedy)

"Let the beauty you are, be what you do"

Every individual is interconnected in beauty. To see beauty, we observe them nonjudgmentally by asking ourselves what are they feeling and needing and doing. We do this by connecting with our bodies, our senses, and with our cognitive empathy (using our thinking, feelings, research, and understanding of science).

Wild Walks help us pause and see how we walk in beauty - the beauty within (Emotional Intelligence) connected to the beauty in other humans (Social intelligence), connected to the beauty in other species (Multispecies Intelligence), connected to the beauty of relationships (Ecological Intelligence), connected to the beauty that is beyond words or thought (Spiritual Intelligence). All these intelligences build upon and contribute to each other, all of which we use to affirm beauty during the walk, intentionally at first with guided practices, and then let our scientific, naturalist, and chattering selves go wild. Human nature is inherently wild, but we too often over over domesticate it with cognitive loops entrenched in culture's stories of oppression that diminish worth and beauty.

(continued on next page)

During the Walk

Open to the feelings of yourself and others, such as:

Affection	Engaged	Hopeful	Confident
Excited	Grateful	Inspired	Joyful
Exhilarated	Peaceful	Refreshed	Afraid
Annoyed	Aversion	Confused	Disconnected
Disquiet	Fatigue	Pain	Embarrassed
Sad	Tense	Yearning	Vulnerable
Other?			

Open to the needs of yourself and others, such as:

Autonomy	Meaning	Connection
Play	Sexual activity	Physical Well-being
Health	Comfort	Adequate nutrition
Satiation	Adequate environment	Safety
Space	Behavior choices	Pleasure
Stimulation	Choice	Use of senses and body
Nurturing young, self/others		Peace
Vitality	Other?	

The Walk Begins and Ends in Beauty

1. Before you walk, breathe deep, stretch arms out, look up, twirl, bow, touch the ground

2. Throughout walk use your senses – smell, hear, see, taste, touch

3. Say, "I walk with beauty before, behind, above, below, all around and in me. It begins in beauty."

4. Begin with the beauty in yourself. Ask, "What am I feeling and needing?" Still your thoughts. Find one feeling/emotion/body state and the need that these feelings are connected to. Fill in one feeling and need word (from list above) and say, No wonder I'm feeling _____. I'm needing _____. Now imagine that need being met. (If thoughts of these needs not being met come up, breathe deep, repeat the "No wonder" statement, and give yourself space to mourn. Repeat this if necessary for all steps)

5. Stop, breathe, stretch, look up, bow

6. With someone you are walking with, share what you are feeling and needing, and say, "No wonder you are feeling _____, you are needing _____." If by yourself, pick someone you are well pleased with and say, "No wonder they are feeling _____ —they are needing _____." If able, repeat with whom you are neutral, and then those with whom you are not pleased. Imagine them having those needs met.

7. Stop, breathe, stretch, look up, bow.

8. Now find another being along the path – plant, tree, mushroom, insect, bird, mammal. If they are moving, walk along side of them if it doesn't bother them, or stand watching. If they are low, go low. Get on the ground if they are really low. Then be them. Move like them. See what they are doing. Guess what they are feeling and needing. Say, "No wonder they are feeling _____, they are needing _____." Imaging them having those needs met.

9. Stop, breathe, stretch, look up. Bow.

10. Now look at all of nature around you. How many species do you see? How are they interacting with each other? Find as many 1:1 relationships as you can. Can you find 3 individuals that are connected to each other? What does each need? Are the relationships harmful? Beneficial? No matter, what does each need and feel? Say as many "no wonders" as you can.

11. Stop, breathe, stretch, look up, bow all around

12. Continue walking now, observing and being. If any thoughts come up, breathe deep and let them go. Walk in silence, smile if you can, saying, "No wonder the world is as it is, because everything is interconnected in beauty, harm, benefit, and tragedy."

13. Stop, breathe, stretch, look up, bow.

14. Say, "I walk with beauty all around me. It is finished in beauty."

For more information: www.oneearthconservation.org

Connecting to One Earth Conservation

This discussion guide is produced by One Earth Conservation (One Earth) as a means to serve you, and hence serve life. We hope it has been nurturing to you and yours. We'd love to hear how these guides nurtured you and how you might use this experience in the future (you can contact us at info@oneearthconservation.org). We plan to produce another edition, and other resources, for the work and joy that is necessary for all of humanity. Would you like to be part of our team? Let us tell you more about One Earth so you can decide.

One Earth Conservation is a U.S.-based 501(c)(3) not-for-profit organization seeking to heal human systems that diminish individual worth and separates humans artificially from the rest of nature in many ways. We affirm that people must be healthy and develop multiple intelligences so all of life, individuals, and human and biotic systems can flourish. One Earth's mission is building knowledge, motivation, resilience, and capacity in people, organizations, and communities in the United States and internationally so that they can better cherish and nurture themselves, nature, and other beings. This is achieved by combining work directed outward toward other beings (our conservation work with parrots in the Americas) and outward towards nature with work directed inward toward one's own human nature (our Nurture Nature Program), as outer well-being and inner well-being are inseparable and mutually beneficial. One Earth invites people into a vision and practice of *interbeing*, based on:

1. All individuals of all species have inherent worth and dignity (all bodies are beautiful, have worth, and matter).
2. All individuals of all species are connected to each other in worth, beauty and well-being.
3. We are also connected in harm. There is no beauty without tragedy. What is done to another, is done to all of us.
4. Embracing this reality, humans grow in belonging to this wondrous planet and the life upon it, and so embraced and nurtured, can nurture in return.
5. This reality of interbeing makes us both powerful and vulnerable, therefore, we need each other to grow and to heal as much as possible.
6. Humans are adaptable and can change, both individually and as families, organizations, communities, and societies. We can become more effective and joyful nurturers and "naturers." This is hard, deep, intentional, and a lifetime's work.

To join our team, you can sign up for our e-newsletter, where we report on our work in the world with endangered parrots in the Americas and list upcoming events and activities. We have a Nurture Nature Academy in which you can enroll for a guided exploration of connection to nature and other species. We also enjoy working with volunteers who seek to serve life through One Earth, such as by helping with organizational growth, social media, and conservation. For more information, visit http://www.oneearthconservation.org.

Thank you, for being you and for being engaged,
Codirectors LoraKim Joyner and Gail Koelln

The Authors

Rev. LoraKim Joyner, DVM: LoraKim combines her experience as a wildlife veterinarian, Unitarian Universalist minister, and Certified Trainer in Nonviolent Communication to address the importance of both human and nonhuman well being in living a deeply meaningful and vibrant life, as well as caring for self, family, relationships, organizations, and life all around us. She serves as a Community Minister affiliated with the Community Unitarian Universalist Church at White Plains, and Co-Director of One Earth Conservation. As an adjunct professor at the Meadville Lombard Theological School, LoraKim teaches "Multispecies and Ecological Ministry, Theology, and Justice" and "Compassionate Communication." She is an inspiring speaker, leading workshops and webinars all over the country in Compassionate Communication and Nurturing Nature. With over 30 years of experience working in Latin America, LoraKim currently leads projects in Guatemala, Honduras, Nicaragua, Guyana, and Paraguay. You can read about her life and work in her memoir, *Conservation in Time of War*.

Gail Koelln, MS: For as long as she can remember, animals have nurtured Gail through their beauty and wonder, and she loves to care for them. As a child, Gail was inspired by Jane Goodall and wanted to grow up to be a zoologist like her. She earned a Master's degree in Zoology, but for various reasons left the field. However, over many years Gail volunteered for the Wildlife Conservation Society, NYC Sierra Club, Gotham City Networking (leading their Gotham Green group), and Climate Reality Project. As a grant writing professional for more than 20 years, she has worked with a number of animal welfare, wildlife, and environmental organizations. After Gail met LoraKim in 2014, she finally found her life's work serving as the Co-Director of One Earth Conservation.

Made in the USA
Middletown, DE
09 March 2020